RoadKill

Hannah
Stay Beautiful
Be happy
Be well
Chris

RoadKill

"you will allways end up where your suposto to be, when its your time to 'stay there!

CHRIS CHRISTIE

Copyright © 2009 by Chris Christie.

Library of Congress Control Number:		2009902920
ISBN:	Hardcover	978-1-4415-2355-6
	Softcover	978-1-4415-2354-9

All rights reserved. No part of this book may be reproduced or transmitted in any form or by any means, electronic or mechanical, including photocopying, recording, or by any information storage and retrieval system, without permission in writing from the copyright owner.

This book was printed in the United States of America.

To order additional copies of this book, contact:
Xlibris Corporation
1-888-795-4274
www.Xlibris.com
Orders@Xlibris.com
60809

IN MEMORY OF JAMES HUFFMAN

For Beth and Amanda
Without whose love and support none of this would be possible

Introduction

I wrote RoadKill while attending the Creative Writing program at Chester College of New England. It utilizes forms that cross disciplines within the scope of Creative Writing. Poetry, memoir, and even fictional elements in the form of metaphor were thrown into the mix. This came about as an organic occurrence and was not a premeditated strategy. Basically, I was making it up as I went along. Some might call this the employment of talent, where understanding the process of creation becomes irrelevant.

To typecast the piece as a whole I would have to put it in the realm of "creative nonfiction." Interpretations of "creative nonfiction" vary, but my own understanding of the genre is that the use of creative nonfiction allows an author the freedom to rely heavily on metaphor, simile, and surrealism to convey those elements within a true story that are intangible or do not exist within the physical world, most notably in the conveyance of emotion, states of mind, and the author's need to relay personal perception of events and ideas to his or her audience. It allows for the gray to show through where traditional nonfiction tends to be black and white.

I started the project in a notebook before I knew anything more about writing than what I remembered from high school. *RoadKill* had been ten years in the making when I enrolled at Chester College of New England in 2004, and it was my primary reason for attending. At different times throughout the process I literally wrote myself into states of physical illness, despair, madness, and the mental fatigue of constant introspection.

I can not dismiss the element of therapeutic value that goes hand in hand with a project such as this, and I can not begin to describe the emotional challenges I faced in writing it. The first sentence of the original draft opens, "I sit on my porch as tears stream down my face, looking out into the trees, hoping that what unfolds before you will some day do for someone what fate has done for me." I see the scope of this work as the product of many tears. It is an embodiment of suffering.

When I started writing *RoadKill* only four years had passed since "The Accident," the central event in my story. My wounds, both physical and emotional, were not yet healed, but I had this thing inside me and had to get it out; if not for others to read, then because I had to step outside myself, so I could be sure that I understood (and even believed) the series of events that led to *RoadKill*

I struggled to get the words on paper. I was driven to madness in the process, and at times I had to close the notebook and keep it hidden from my sight. My hope was that through my story I might lend someone else the courage to fight when all else has failed them.

I held onto the idea that I was writing it for reasons greater than myself. The thought urged me on. Forty-six hand-written pages and one massive manic breakdown later, I had done it.

I rewrote my story on a computer and stored it on a 3.5" floppy disk. At that time I had no choice but to forget about the notebook and disk. My sanity depended on it. Not only did the notebook contain my story, but I also wrote extensively about heartache and the loss of god. In other words, it was literally the diary of a madman and the story of what drove him mad. The parts of the book that revealed the truth about me were seemingly as crazy as the rest of the psychobabble it contained. I was literally told by a psychiatrist, "no more notebooks." I was forbidden to write. My mania had gotten to the point that my wife became visibly nervous at the sight of me with a pen in my hand. It now seems ironic that I went on to pursue a degree in Creative Writing.

With school in session I began adding to my story's fragile beginnings. Some of my earliest English Comp. essays were about my experiences in the hospital, but at the time I didn't realize they would eventually work their way into the project. I kept the work I had done and the work I was doing as two separate entities. When I finally figured out my essays could easily be edited to fit into the body of the original story I began to form a strategy for putting some meat on its bones. That meant I had to go back into the notebook. I approached the project with caution and fear. It had been about eight years since I had opened the notebook. I kept it hidden at the bottom of a box wrapped up in a hospital Johnny.

Luckily I found a computer that could still read the obsolete 3.5" floppy disk. In my spare time between studying hard and creating art I started working on the project again in small steps, adding bits, pieces, and sometimes entire essays. Sophomore year it began to grow, and I found the more I was adding the more I needed to add. Everything I wrote seemed to need a back story, so I started filling in all the blanks. One of my first challenges was to figure out what (or, more appropriately, what not) to include. It became an albatross, and I lost sight of its boundaries. Instead of a story centered on an event in my life it was becoming my entire life.

I knew I wanted to write a story that didn't fall into the "self help" genre. I tried to avoid preachy moments of advice. Who wants to feel talked at when reading a story? I wanted it to fit into something in terms of literary context, whatever that turned out to be. At first I relied heavily on lessons in fiction writing to guide me. The works of Raymond Carver, Grace Paley, and David Crouse were among my earliest studied authorial styles. Alice McDermott's, *That Night,* stands out for me as a lesson in the dynamics of narration. In brief there are three narrators; me, myself, and I, all associated with my own past, present, and future, and I could slip into and out of their individual or collective knowledge. McDermott did it so well. I see her book as a memoir, wrapped in a story, surrounded by a legend, told by a narrator assuming three postures of the first person: she who saw what happened, she who heard what happened, and she with clairvoyant insightfulness because the third "I" is privy to the other's experiences. Often, what results is a version of the facts that are contrived from speculation, the narrator's intuition. McDermott makes no attempt to hide these techniques or make them seem as a quirky gimmick, but allows them to come out as an organic part of how the story is told—the random connections a mind makes as it goes through the process of recount and recall.

In studying forms of fiction I was able to get a feel for my own style and form. It was through studying fiction that I grew to appreciate and learned to manipulate the various mechanisms I used in *RoadKill:* metaphor, foreshadowing, narration and nonlinear forms.

Poetry became the next element to find its way into "The Story". My poem, *The Candy Striper,* was inserted directly into the text in its full narrative form. Again, this was an organic occurrence. Throughout my course of schooling I wrote six poems about my experiences with death and the hospital. Five of them are used in the story's text, although because their forms were not readily made in narrative prose, they could not always be utilized verbatim. In another coincidental mishap, the first section reads almost like an epic, though it was written as a memoir. Throughout the revision process I remained conscious of such elements as consonance, rhythm, and music as I shaped my work. The following passage demonstrates use of the letter "W." I think it helps to capture the likeness of what my ride was like, although that is ultimately an interpretation for readers to see for themselves:

> "Wind and vibration beat my body into exhaustion; the wind was never at my back. The weather was unusually cold, cold enough that my hands would stiffen to the handle grips. But I was used to riding in the cold weather of New England." (32)

It was my intent to produce a piece of work that created solid visual and emotional connections for the reader, and I think poetry helped that along. I do not consciously subscribe to any particular school of thought when it comes to poetry, so I can not point to particular influences in my work other than to say my work became the sum of my experiences. I think the study of Ezra Pound and his Ideogrammatic Method fit nicely into what I was trying to do. Like Pound, my writing utilizes imagery, and tends to be direct and to the point. Although metaphor does come through in my work, I don't think there are any great mysteries as to how it all fits into the piece as a whole. I try not to hide inside lofty vocabulary or circular arrangements. I think that's where the "power" of my writing lies. It is easily accessible in a way that face value becomes all that is necessary to understand what I am trying to relay.

My own voice dominates my writing, so I do not find the need for emulation. The most valued influences in my work are from writers I've had the privilege of working with during my four years at CCNE. Poet Pam Bernard, whose guidance fostered the success of "The Candy Striper," was instrumental in helping me shape my writing around my voice. The poetry of visiting writer Diana Lee Veelee was a big influence on my own writing. Her work also dealt with personal trauma, and through it I found something to relate to in my own writing.

It would not be right to speak of my writing or the success of this project without giving credit to the influence literary artist Jenn Monroe has had on my work.

It was Professor Monroe's mentoring that shaped what became of my writing. From its raw beginnings where I had trouble staying in a consistent tense, to my more skilled work, where tense was still an issue. Throughout the scope of the project, I played with tense changes and struggled to use my tense-challenged mind as a deliberate mechanism within the story.

At times I had to rewrite and revise large blocks of work as different "tense" strategies proved ineffective for the story. I found that sometimes the best way to figure out what will work is to try everything that doesn't work first. In other words, don't be afraid to make a lot of mistakes. Originally, the story bounced from past to present tense, sometimes several times in a single scene. It made sense to me, but from the readers POV, it wasn't translating as well. I think I was over working McDermott's model of narration. With much coaching from Prof. Monroe, it ended up being so much simpler than I was trying to make it. The format worked itself out to be—present tense, past tense, present tense, past tense. The segments in present tense create an intimate closeness where I intended to transpose intense emotion, and the past tense sections provide a break from that intensity. It serves as a chance for the reader to detach from immediacy of the action. As a result, I've been told that it is a fast read, and easy to stay engaged in the text.

It was through memoir that the story propelled itself from an uncertain collection of various avenues and ideas to a vision of the finished product.

In studying authors such as Frank McCourt, Primo Levi, and Henry Miller I was able to flush out the introduction section of *RoadKill*. It started as a memoir piece titled *The Last Disciple*, and with it came something for the story to return to in the end. With this short, I saw a new light for "The Story." I realized the importance of the struggle inside myself if I was going to write it as true to life as I could convey. The element of mental anguish had to play as important a role as the physical accident. I now had a full circle to come around to, and this greatly helped resolve the context which the timeframe of events would occur. In other words, the story would begin and end with me sitting in the same place going crazy. It's essentially a mind warp that the reader is led through. Another memoir short titled *Humility Dump*, also written through the memoir class, was inserted into the story, almost entirely in its original form.

At this point it had become easier to work on the project, but I was still struggling to overcome the emotion associated with having to relive the ordeal every time I sat down to write. There were times when I would rather have abandoned it altogether. I would become ill, break down crying, and then have to recover from the depression that followed. I often asked myself "Why."

The writing process was surreal at times, and surrealism plays a large part of what I ask the reader to believe in the story. "Not everything is as it seemed." I make that point early on in the piece. Much of what transpired in my story happened either inside my mind, or outside of the physical world. Trying to convey those moments was frightening, to say the least. I had to address the question of how to transpose the emotion of something that wasn't happening, but was. The tenets of surrealism provide for the acknowledgment that the dream state exists as reality, and having lived through my own virtual nightmare I understood exactly how the surrealists came up with that idea. In the book I try to describe it as (to borrow a theme from Henny Penny) "Just because the sky isn't really falling doesn't mean it won't hurt when pieces of it hit your head."

As the project developed, I still had no clue about how to relate to it in terms of its literary context. To say it was a memoir piece didn't quite fit into what I had written, and yet it wasn't a full blown autobiography either. The closest I could get was to say that it was creative nonfiction. It wasn't until studying the works of Fydor Dostoevsky, Vladimir Nabokov, and Johann Wolfgang von Goethe that I found some semblance of context in which my story fell. I could relate to the characters they created. I found the shared idea of "transparency" in relation to humanity in both Nabokov's *Invitation to a Beheading*, and my own story. I saw bits and pieces of myself in Goethe's *The Sorrows Young Werther*, and this helped to tune in on the element of my own story that deals with madness. Even the character Darl in Faulkner's *As I lay Dying* helped to place my own character (me) in a literary context. It wasn't that I brought the ideas and writing of these authors into my work, but a greater understanding of their works in general helped to give my story direction as it approached the later stages of development. It also seemed fitting to include imagery with the story. In today's scandalous nonfiction genre it helps to provide a bit of documentation wherever one can. I've found this to be true in retelling the story verbally as well. People have doubted it from my own mouth. As mentioned in the beginning of this essay, even I needed to understand and believe the series of events.

When senior year started the project was well under way. I was at the point where all I had to do was bridge gaps between the various essays and segments I'd inserted over the past few years. The page count quickly doubled. My tense issues were still haunting me, but eventually they were brought into agreement. It was a long run of reading it over from beginning to end, inserting, deleting, and correcting as I went along. I literally drew from everything I learned in four years of college, from students and professors alike. As I mentioned earlier my work is the sum of my experiences, and that is how my story was assembled. I threw everything in there.

At the final pass through it all I dug deeper into the accident's eye witness accounts and operative reports for any information that would enhance the story. Adding actual medical terminology and specifics about the extent of injuries and treatments was helpful in relaying authenticity. Adding the real names of some of the professionals who cared for me helped add a touch of personality to the piece. It was a nod of recognition for their professionalism and expertise, without which I highly doubt I'd have lived to tell the tale. I can say with certainty that there are names I should have mentioned in the book, but memory is involuntarily selective; this in no way diminishes the importance of their presence in my life. Let me just end it on this note. To the excellent people at Halifax Medical Center in Daytona Beach who crossed my path in the spring of 1994—I'll never forget you.

These walls are pale and tiled, yellow. A simple single bed draped with stark white bedding is fitted with restraints—padded leather and buckles. My bare feet cold against a hard floor, tiled and polished; the room has all the personality of sand. Bars on the window cast oblique shadows across a chair in the corner. They follow the square padded outline of its cushions—a sharp angle where they pass over a writing desk and reach to the ceiling on the wall behind. The soldiers are gone now, He left too, receding into the milky mist of a daydream, and I sit in a chair, my body Tired and battered.

I search my memory for what brought me to this stone room. Long thick strands of hair hide my face from the cold, vindictive world, and my eyes roll in the back of my head searching for any clue as to how I came to be. I sit in utter confusion.

*   *   *

I begin to tremble, fearful, reality, it's inevitable I'm dying, or perhaps I'm already gone. Wearing nothing but wrapped in an Indian blanket, I press my body flat against the wall beside the great bay window peering into the outside-upside-down world. I'm the last living soul in the aftermath of a nuclear winter. Gray ash falls like flurries—snow from an infinite gray sky.

Ice drums on skylights thirty feet over my head filling the post and beam room with a snare—hell's corpses marching. I drift to the great blizzard of seventy-eight, of the people who died, so many of them buried, suffocating under the crushing feet of snow. Their anguish, alive in me as though it were my own, weighed heavily on my conscience as I lay like death on the couch. Hiding beneath my blanket waiting to be buried, zombetic souls wander aimlessly through a vast Masonic order, hallways of stone; a Minotaur waits in the shadows. I am no Theseus. Raw fear courses through my veins, my blood thickens, magma throbs in my temples and in my neck. I harden.

I move from beneath a woven cocoon, and through the kitchen I pebble the floor with a 30 pound bag of dog food, purification, a bitter taste on my tongue. Standing in the open front doorway, tears stream down my face, ashes fall from a pale gray sky. I cry for the loss of innocence, and I cry for the children with no one to cry for them. For the first time in my life I realize there is no one left to cry for me. Eternal dread walks in my shadow as I wander from the house into the vast silent emptiness. Laughing children stalk me, taunt my name from other dimensions.

He calls to my every deep seeded-fear, fears I never knew existed; He plays them against me in a game of manhunt that began with the forming of time and will end in this day and age, of which I was once a living part. My existence is caught in time, stuck in limbo. This, this reality, is an afterlife.

Wandering into the cavernous day, I cry my way across the street in a state of perpetual despair to lower my neighbor's flag from its mast. I confront the kind old man who I admired as a child growing up. A neighborhood hero—retired, a Lieutenant in the Fire Department. Everyone loved Fred. His face is old and pale, the strength I saw in it as a boy has left him.

My coming is prophetic of death.

"Don't go in there, you can't go in there," he exclaims, grabbing at the lapels of my black full-length oil-skin duster.

"It's all right, Fred, you're just having a heart attack!" I hold Fred by the wrists and twist his hand loose. I climb the stairs to his living room seeking sanctuary on the couch. Lying supine, arms crossed at the chest, I take the rigor pose of death and beg him to cover me with his flag. Exhaustion—I need refuge, sanctuary. Someplace to close my eyes, where my mind can hide from Him. He who relentlessly pushes from within stopping at nothing, ignoring pain, driving me to places I am never prepared to go. I just want to sleep forever.

He never sleeps.

He picks me up and throws me like a rag-doll into an alien world of uncertainty. Family and friends I once knew are scattered as dust over the land. My purpose for seeking refuge here becomes ever clearer, however little sense it makes. My mind travels a barren landscape in search of any fragment of familiarity. My mission clear—acquire the key; expose it all for the sham of a bloodstained vendetta that it is.

The world is at war and life goes by for the jaded masses as though there are roses in every garden. I'm sickened by humanity. Am I the only one punished? Why am I made to suffer? Why must I be their strength? Weakness bleeds from my pores so I might watch it bead and roll down my mangled limbs, unable to shake it away. I've been awake for days. The ghost of time floating, my senses; He keeps me guessing at every turn. Pain reminds me every day I'm not dead, it grounds me, shows me the earth is still firm beneath my feet. But I am numb, euphoric, spiraling through heaven and hell. Pain has forgotten me, and anguish remains in its place. I feel nothing.

An officer escorts me from Fred's house—it is my calling to put a bullet in this officer's head and then one in mine so that we will not live on earth as the last two beings left to go mad in the holocaust. Inside his car is like a capsule. This is it, this is what it comes down to, and I brace myself in anticipation, relishing the moment that we achieve light speed. It never arrives. "Docs this thing have warp drive?"

I am led through a labyrinth, my eyes fix on his sidearm, and I see it happen in a flash. We stand ankle deep in frozen ash, crying in each other's arms, longtime friends saying a last goodbye as I pull the trigger once, then again. *I* facilitate the extinction of humanity.

They lock me in a cage of concrete and steel. I think of nothing other than *I know they will make me ride the lightning for what I have done,* but I can't recall what that might have been. From behind the eyes of a lunatic, I flush my glasses down the stainless commode.

He sees it all with perfect clarity—*Can't use those where You're going*

My soul cyclones through my entrails, reeling toward a vortex that sucks my essence from inside the bowl. I struggle to surface while sinking deeper into a destiny that never should have come this far. I take off my sweat pants and soak them in the water then wildly slap them against the bars, the walls. This place is filth, purification, and the taste in my mouth is bitter. Plexiglass between the heavy, black bars and me. Beyond them, a narrow hallway, voices of torment rise and circle like the last brittle leaves of Autumn in a whip of December wind, Dante's wailing soul. A dog snarls, I hear its claws scratching into the cement floor.

I touch the inferno.

I'm naked in the cold cell, a stainless steel shelf on the wall, and I expect death to take me, accept that it will, I must go with nothing more than what I was given at birth. Sirens burst loudly in my ears. In and out of life, I try to make sense of what I see and hear around me. I've been beaten badly but hang on. I try not to breathe, knowing that my next breath might bring the hollow rasping moan, my last.

An officer takes my arm; I rise. He leads me down the hallway where there was no dog snarling, only a man at a desk holding up my duster. "Don't you want to put this on?" I spin the oily coat around my naked shoulders, arms falling through the sleeves, coarse on my bare flesh. They lead me down a series of hallways into the garage. I see myself here as a child inflating my bicycle tires. I expect to be placed in the trunk of the car and shot. I am bold, willing to accept this fate.

I hear voices, hands touch my body. Background, sounds of electronic gadgetry blip and squelch. I'm still in a place of this earth. But how? I died so long ago. An excited voice exclaims, "We're losing him," and I slip into a state of consciousness from which I have no desire to return. Like falling through fiber-optics I speed in and out of time. Instinct is all I have to free me from my chains. My mind is out of time, in an ambulance fighting for life. My body, out of place, shackled on the floor of a Plymouth County Sheriff's van, I'm screaming for justice. Tin voices talk about me over the radio, Weïrd Sisters cackling. I gasp for air. The Sisters prod my head with large wooden paddles; my face sinks beneath the cauldron.

I'm a prisoner in a strange place without a notion why. Instinct takes over and I become both predator and victim. *Remain calm, show no emotion, do not give into fear, do not go down without a fight.* In a world of uncertainty, chance favors the fighter, and He acts freely inside me but within His own mind. Where did this advice come from? I can't remember hearing the words, but they're on top of my mind as instinctively as sex.

I am the prey, He the hunter, and the cage is our range. If they take me, it will only be for their numbers. I coil in fear to draw them in, and then He awakens. He dares them all to pull me, rip me from these bars that they themselves fear the most. Within each of my captors are secrets so deep that in hell they may be played on for an eternity as the tragedy that was their life on earth. Backed into a corner He's ready to fight. He looks for their secrets, for the exposed flesh of tender underbellies.

He taunts them from my cage, baits them, and exposes them. This will be a battle they will not soon forget, and in the end my only solace will be that they will never forget the spirit within me—the brown, almond eye of the Rottweiler.

He tears at the chain with his teeth, but my wrists remain bound.

If I could just win the war, the war that rages on inside me. Amman Rae has banished me from his lighted chasms—even he was unable to take me. I cling to knowing there can be no demise without an end, but it never ends.

I am in and out of death. Angels of mercy whisper breezes of life while around me are distorted images of what is now and what has been. They bind me through two states of existence, one familiar somewhat comfortable, the other more distant, unknown, but preferable. Which is the one created for me? Why have they brought me to this place? They all watch me, intensely scrutinizing my every move. I must be cold; I must be impartial if I must live. Who are they to bathe my every wound in salt? I must be cold. They all lie. In another life I was strong, a being of honor and independence. Here I am weak, vulnerable, and volatile.

I lay alone contemplating destiny while the shadows on the wall whisper to me in voices I remember hearing as a child. They call to me trying to break my spirit, and they are all around me. *Remember us? Remember how you trembled at night in bed and how you befriended us to hide your fright? We are still here, and you still tremble.* I sit in the corner—the only place the camera can't look through me. Chains rattle from somewhere while the voices whisper amongst themselves and laugh. I must find where they are vulnerable, the one brick that will give, the one wound that will close itself over, leaving their faces dower in disbelief of what they know to be the only true given factor which steers them blindly through life. For Him it is the simplest of equations, logical, precise, and predictable. It comes to me so clearly now. For them it remains a mystery to be seen. The Shadows are silent now. I have mastered all that surrounds me. I call upon the Shadows, drawing life from their emptiness. I am my own last disciple and I know the consequences if I lose. Now, externally in stasis, I draw back. Left alone in silence to graze my wounds, the walls close ever tightly around me and I choke to stay alive in my own omnipotence. I call out from within my mind but hear only the madman's prophecy.

He screams at them from behind the bars, calling them by names, targeting something about them:

> *Mister Green Jeans,*
> *Fat Slob,*
> *Hey Old Man!*

—slaves that they are. He pushes buttons playing head-games with soldiers. One of them retorts, I have a code name among them—a guard dubs me Captain Outrageous.

If they are to have me as their captive, He will set the pace—it's a game to Him, for He is that in me of which I am most afraid. He is that part of me who will kill to live, driven by a disciplined fury, and always awake inside me. He is the student of war, a master of strategy, a weapon with only one objective—survival.

I untie my black combat boots and throw them through the bars. My boots are off, I'm barefoot; what are they waiting for? I throw money at them citing its meaninglessness, taunting, "come and take me now," daring them to get close enough. My boot laces are cuffed in the palm of my hand. He wants to kill them.

In god we trust!—Epluribus Unum!
Bullshit!
You are all fucking sheep!
One fool confronts Him at the edge of the cage.

"Put your arms outside the bars," he dares me, and I do, but I notice the glint of handcuffs loosely concealed by the pawn's side. I swipe at the fool with a grizzly's paw, and the man turns to the others proclaiming, "He hit me!"

But I missed.

You're a lying fucking sheep at that!
I hear Him wanting inside my head, wanting someone to open the door, to come inside my cell where He waits patiently. The feel of boot-strings in His hand soothes Him. He paces, breathing heavily through my moist nostrils, and howls to the voices a cry of war.

"CHEROCKEEEEEEEEEE"
He wails the names of forgotten friends, a voice that crackled over the radio from far away, a last surviving warrior. The names of people and places cycle through His memory as He tries in desperation to make relevant connections between yesteryear and today. He circles the cage like a rabid animal knocking on the wall every six inches until at last one of the bricks answers. It is hollow—a weak link in their chain. He hammers on it with my fragile fist. To start a hole, we must first dig.

He paces the cell, biding time, storing energy, soaking His head in the toilet to keep Himself alert—awake—sucking the water off the ends of his hair to stay hydrated. He stands at the door striking the lock-box with his fist screaming at them in riddles, talking circles around their simple minds, talking us both into exhaustion.

Six of them come through the door at once and bind my limbs with chains while He is quiet, and I am exhausted, my head hangs down. Neither of us see them coming. Mr. Green Jeans binds my legs while Fat Slob and the old man hold my arms. The other three secure manacles to my scarred wrists.

Languidly, hindered by chains, they escort their prisoner through the hallway. If I'm to survive, He must be shrewd. Where are they leading me? I'm unsure if He was still on earth as the stench of a thousand forgotten souls loomed heavy in the air. I walk slowly. We pass beneath a series of portraits that look like sadistic school-marms. The one in the middle could have been the person responsible for Rose Kennedy's lobotomy.

Sardonically, He takes comfort in knowing they are clumsy at His pace, and possibly one of them will trip, leaving me an opportunity. But to do what? The thought of them falling excites Him, He waits for opportunity. I hold my head low allowing my hair to restrict the line of sight from their eyes to His. There are still six of them, all in uniform, all armed. He calculates the moves it will take to disarm and dispose of them all.

What crime am I guilty of? Wild speculations as to where I am and what possible fate lies in the darkness spiral throughout my head as they guide me through each new doorway. He hears the keys and the bolts unlocking then locking again.

With the rhythmic precision of a Nazi precession they make their way in and out of an architectural labyrinth. The cadence of their boot heels break only for the occasional command for me to "look foreword," "don't speak." He counts my steps and tracks each turn. When I need him, He will know the way out. They fear His gaze. They pray it not fall upon them, for they are vulnerable to their own weaknesses. He knows the way inside their heads and how to instill in them the very fear and every pain that I had been ignoring since the day I was sentenced in hell to this life on earth.

* * *

A woman sits facing me. She motions to my captors—they recede. Behind her is a young man built like a marine, right down to the haircut. He stretches a pair of latex gloves over his hands and glares at me inhospitably. I rub my wrists, badly bruised, purple from the shackles that bound me only moments before.

"You are the first person that's ever had an armed escort all the way up here," she explains.

"It cuts the skin." I rub my wrists gouged by the shackles. Through my stringy hair I can see parts of her face. She is gentle, her eyes kind, she is strong, wise. I part my hair with my fingers and feel myself again.

"Yea, they'll do that to you," she replies. "This is Mark," He coldly nods his head uncrossing his arms. They hang by his side like loaded guns.

"My name's Charlene, I'm a registered nurse." She seems not to be hiding anything.

"My name's Chris. I don't know if I exactly agree with *this*." I point to Mark standing behind her, to the bed, and restraints. I suppress Him as he nags in the back of my head, *Mark must fall on first strike—no second chances.*

She laughs, "You're not stupid . . . confused maybe, but not stupid." She signals the strong arm and he removes the restraints from the bed. "We're not going to need *these*." She looks at me with severity, trust, *"are we?"*

Be careful what you wish for, or so the saying goes. I was forever struggling, working two and sometimes three jobs, living week to week with empty pockets. Alcohol was my escape, but it offered no reprieve. I labored just to keep my head above water, but I was drowning. I knew there had to be an easier way, and in the back of my thoughts I fantasized about being in an accident.

I moved out of my parents' house on my eighteenth birthday. By the time I was 20 I was married and had a child; we named her Amanda. We purchased a two-family house. It was too much for a young kid to have on his shoulders.

Somewhere in the confusion I bought my first bike, a Harley Davidson, 1990, 1200 Sportster, brand new, black with orange script on the tank. It looked just like the drawing I did that hung over my bedroom door as a kid. I fouled a few spark plugs and ran out of gas once or twice. I even ran into a moving car, but I became a weather-hardened four-season-rider. I didn't own a car, didn't want one, couldn't afford one if I did. Besides, a cage was an oppressive concept.

I checked out the bike club scene, never understood it, and never wore a patch. I couldn't get past the fact that in a group of about 250 "bikers" there was a clique of about a dozen that wore the "1%" patch denoting them as one-percenters: a term to reference lone wolves, people with little need for social structures. One generally does not fall into the category through self proclamation.

They all wore the same patches in the same places on their vests—D I L L I G A F (do I look like I give a fuck)—but they all seemed to be opinionated. I wasn't a follower of the idea of tying my identity to the back of a black leather jacket with thread, but I dressed in black with all the belt-clipped accessories to complete the look: the cigarette pouch, knife, and chain. I wore my face like armor. It was the only part of me not wrapped in leather when I found myself vulnerable in strange places. I had the attitude and the ugly face. That face bikers wear idling at red lights while trying to be harder than flesh and bone. That face that said *FUCK YOU!* to anyone bold enough to glance at it.

I turned my lifestyle into an ideal because there were no means to do it differently. It was easier to discount the unobtainable than to reach for it. As far as I was concerned, there was me, my machine, and the road beneath my tires—my road, a place no one else could occupy. As long as I had gas, the road was always there for me.

Although mingling with the biker element, there was no sense of camaraderie for me. There were no "brothers in the wind," or a need to raise my hand and wave for every fool who leapt off his saddle to wave at me from the opposite lane. Occasionally I would find myself eyeballing a rider who was eyeballing me. A short quick nod of the head was all that was necessary to acknowledge that we understood the road in the same solemn way.

Motorcycles became just machines to me, simplistic things that could be had by anyone with a dollar and decent credit. If you've seen one, you've seen them all. With exception to variations of style, they were all internal combustion engines splashed with paint, chrome, and ego. I was seduced by it all at first, but it didn't take more than one trip to Laconia during Bike Week to realize that the art of motorcycle enthusiasm was a social disease whose victims congregate in masses and gawk slack jawed at motorcycles the way simple school-girls might show interest in shiny new shoes. These were weekend warriors, the people who thought that buying a motorcycle and new leather made them a "biker." They weren't. They towed their machines around on trailers and were lucky if they had a few thousand miles in the saddle. They hunkered under over-passes in the rain as I sped by laughing with stinging bullets of water piercing my flesh, the pain a kick, like too much caffeine.

I became lost in the wind. Seduced like Ulysses to the sirens. I left my wife for a sinking ship of an older married woman. I never figured out if it was the motorcycle or me she lusted for, but she was a quick way out of the mistake I'd made in marrying at 19. I'd proven the entire world right; my marriage had lasted barely two years.

It was too easy, the way it all fell in place. "I was young, dumb, and full of cum," as the saying goes. I was 21, she was 30. She kicked her husband out of their apartment, and I moved in the next day. I was getting laid like I had only ever seen in the raunchiest of pornographic movies. I couldn't believe it was happening to me. I was in love.

Ultimately, this move alienated me from my friends and family. It seemed like everyone had an opinion about it, and that opinion was never in my favor. People said the motorcycle changed me and was turning me into an asshole. My poor wife—they all sympathized with her, took her side. Fuck them all. I was following my own path, and if that meant loosing friends, I was willing to make that move. I was weary of doing what I thought others wanted me to do. I was sick of doing things for no other reason than it was what people expected. It took both of us to create the mess, but no, *I* was the asshole because I drank heavily.

At the time, a three-bedroom apartment was in the seven hundred dollar range. My girlfriend and I were living week to week. Between our bar tab, her Bingo habit, and her two ungrateful bastards, there was nothing left by Sunday but hangovers. Child support was eating my wages to where I couldn't afford to live on my own. We never seemed to get ahead, and every time we thought there was something extra, something else went wrong that tapped out funds, usually vehicle repairs.

I worked hard, always had. I started young, finding lawns to mow and paper routes. I hustled for money; it was my one redeeming quality. They could say plenty about me, but not that I didn't work for a living. At fourteen I was working in an auto glass shop where I learned how to party, and then landed in Narcotics Anonymous. From there I worked long hours in the hot kitchens of two Greek restaurants. I learned the bones of the business from Nick-O, a hard man, a friend. From there I learned how to build a business from the ground up as First Cook for a Greek named Art.

After getting married I needed the security of paid sick days, available overtime, and raises, so I started working in the hellfire of corporate nursing homes. I went to work every day dressed in white. Through thankless hours and a grueling routine, I managed to work my way up to director of food services and began to feel the effects of burn-out.

There was sadness and death all around me. Residents came and went. The desperately lonely were always waiting in the halls to tell me about a visit from a son or daughter I knew was never coming. Those who had lost their minds long ago tugged at my shirt tails from their chairs thinking I was a brother or a lover from long ago. There were constant complaints from the same people about the same issues all the time, some of them legitimate, most of them foolishness. Everyone working for me seemed to be giving 100 percent, but it was never good enough. Administration wanted more than I could give. It was thankless work.

Typical corporate bureaucracy bullshit led to my getting fired: the paperwork, the regulation, and insider knowledge of what a racket the industry was pulling on the state. Unofficially it happened like this: I was taking a four-day vacation to go fishing with friends when the park ranger came to my camp site and informed me that there was an emergency at work; they expected me to be there. I had no intention of giving up the only time off I had taken in two years. It was requested and approved by the asshole. If my fill-in didn't show up for work, then it was the asshole's job to be there in the kitchen cooking; it was company policy. He wasn't happy when I returned from my trip.

Officially, I was fired when he called me into the office to discuss the weekend, and I voiced my concerns about the administration's idea of corporate ethics. I was told I had a bad attitude. I was burnt out on it all, and was tired of fighting for what's right in an industry that exploits the elderly for bottom-line capitol gain.

"This sucks," I said. I stuck my name tag into the top of his desk and walked. Then the Administrator chased me down the hall as I was leaving and asked if I would stay on staff until he could replace me; I told him I was going to find work breaking someone's legs. He had nothing else to say. After only a few weeks on unemployment I was lucky enough to find another job at a home called the Ocean Manor.

While all this was going on, my girlfriend announced that she had met someone at the VFW bar and wanted to see him again. That meant she was already fucking him. I'd spent the last three years of my life working like a dog helping to support her two brats, and I had nothing. I could have stayed, but she offered to leave. I left with no idea where I was going to go. For the second time in three years I was leaving it all behind. The cycle of deconstruction haunted me.

The bank took my house. I'd racked up a seventy-five-hundred-dollar debt on my credit card, my first one, all of it on the girlfriend. Paying child support hit me hard. With the court garnishing my wages I was taking home less than two bills a week; not much to live on let alone pay rent. I'd let my credit fall out from under me. My days amounted to one big-shitty-snowball rolling downhill toward the rest of my life.

I reluctantly crawled back to my parent's home, sleeping on the floor in a cellar room called "the red room." I moved back in with a piss-warm-half-empty keg of beer and began drinking full time. I didn't want to be there at their house any more than they wanted me there, but I had no options. Each week I spent my last five bucks on draught beer. I'd lost or let everything I ever had slip away from me until there was nothing left but a motorcycle and my daemons.

Later, I returned to the apartment where the ex-girlfriend was still living. Only her son was there, and he let me in. I was too drunk to function and had a 16-year-old girl with me. I projectile vomited all over the bathroom. The next thing I knew I was waking up on the couch, with the police standing over me. Luckily, my younger brother took out after me on his bike that night just to keep an eye open. He'd gotten the jailbait out of there before the cops showed up. Two days later I received a restraining order.

I knew I had to start rebuilding my life. I had lost all self-respect, dignity, and pride. There was nowhere left to go but up, and I needed to be far away from Massachusetts, and sober, if I was going to get there.

I saw the solution to my problem staring at me from the glossy pages of an *E-Z Rider* magazine. Like a sign from the biker god himself, an advertisement for AMI (American Motorcycle Institute) in Florida caught my attention in the summer of '93. I thought about it for a day or two and concluded that my career in restaurant and institutional foodservice was burning me out. I couldn't keep going the way I was, and after a couple of phone calls I was enrolled in AMI's 20-week Harley Davidson program. It was going to be nice to get away from winter. It made perfect sense that if one only has two wheels for transportation, then Florida's the perfect place to be.

I spent my last night in Massachusetts at the Ocean Manor's Christmas party. I fucked a married girl, (my sort of new girlfriend) in the back of her car in the parking lot. I didn't know what it was about married girls. They seemed easy. I was drawn to them for reasons that were beyond my understanding, and it seemed that they just found me when I wasn't looking. She had to get home, so I was stranded at the bar, started walking home, got picked up by a nurse who recognized me, partied at her place some more, and finally got a ride home at around 5 a.m. By 10 a.m. I was on the road to Florida with one of my worst hangovers and a Nor'easter nipping at my tail. I rode like hell.

My entire world was again reduced to one Harley Davidson, and whatever tools, clothes, and necessities I could cram inside two saddlebags and an old army duffle. Except this time, possibilities were present. The road was beneath me, and was my home. I was looking for a new career, a new outlook, and a new life. Who was I kidding? I was running from an old career, a bad outlook, and an empty life, but the further my Sportster carried me from Massachusetts, the easier it was to convince myself that I was doing the right thing.

I had managed to save about fifteen hundred dollars and if careful would have enough money to get myself to Daytona Beach. I would pay for a two-month advance on the room I reserved at the International Inn and still have some left to live on. I was going to find a job when I got there. I had one thing going for me; I was a cook, a job skill useful almost anywhere.

It's not easy work hauling ass down an interstate on a Sportster. The peanut tank with its two gallon capacity had me stopping about once every hour. I carried an extra gallon of gas in my saddlebag to be safe, because I learned the hard way. More than once I'd run the tank dry and had to push the bike, sometimes all night, to find gas. It seemed like I only ran out of gas when I was the furthest distance between two gas stations.

Wind and vibration beat my body into exhaustion; the wind was never at my back. The weather was unusually cold, cold enough that my hands would stiffen to the handle grips. But I was used to riding in the cold weather of New England. I was one of those die-hards you see every now and then riding his Harley through the snow, on the way to work at five a.m. with only a bandana over his face. One of those who fool himself into thinking that he chose the motorcycle—reality being there was no other choice, and the motorcycle chose me. I frowned on riding in a cage, but it's easy to frown on that which is unobtainable, and easier still to ride a motorcycle over the snow using my feet as runners. Florida was looking better by the minute, as the coldness that followed me south was a new kind of cold. It carried with it a dampness that set deep into my joints and hardened my limbs in a saddled posture. At every stop I went through a routine of prying my frozen hands open and retrieving money from my chain-drive wallet. It became a time consuming chore that was only the beginning of a long process. My hands were non-responsive unbuttoning my duster, then the quilt lined flannel. I hoped I didn't look stupid moving in slow motion with a pained look on my face.

Southern hospitality proved to be more of a euphemism than a reality. Rest areas were nervous places where people looked at me with either fear or disdain. Once a trooper eyeballed me suspiciously. I knew he was sizing me up for the bag of weed in my pocket. Grizzled men in checkered flannel seemed to be sneering at me with disgust from beneath the bills of their greasy CAT caps. I walked into a 76 and took a stool at the counter. Waitresses paraded past with one hot dish after the other. They never acknowledged I was there. The fat trucker next to me was grunting over a three-piece chicken dinner, elbowing me as he wiped his mouth on his sleeve. Ten minutes later someone sat two stools down and was waited on. I took the hint. I left hungry.

I learned fast how to read the change of air in a room as I stood inside doorways exhuming my fingers from gauntlets. Everyone looks but no one raises a head. I either felt comfortable or I didn't.

There was nothing to think about except holding on against the wind, which grew colder as the sun faded. My ears full of machine and wind, my mind slipped into places I wished it wouldn't go: thoughts of guilt, my daughter, regret, hope, optimism, I couldn't wait to get to Jacksonville. I needed a drink.

I didn't have the strength to stop in Jacksonville. I finally made it to where 301 split from I-10, and I filled the tank yet again before continuing south. It was a long stretch of desolate dark country—too dark to know what was out there. An occasional small town came and went with little more than a Handy-Way, traffic light, and railroad crossing. Some were not even dots on a map. I was exhausted, and my unfamiliarity with the road made it seem like I had been riding through the night for days. It was my first taste of tropical air and palm. Towns got bigger along the way: Lawtey, Stark, Waldo. A rib shack in the middle of nowhere came and went. I thought about a hot meal, and then it was gone.

In the midst of waiting for the bike to get there, I was dreaming. My body was the road so I could navigate regardless of where my mind went. It had to go somewhere because I couldn't see beyond the headlight; I would see nothing but road for a half-hour. I sang a stupid song I remembered from music class in the fifth grade—"Silent Night" in German. The ride had grown monotonous.

My shoulder! It was suddenly sore as hell. Had it exploded? My hand slipped from the handle grip and I sucked against my clenched teeth trying to stay rigid. Keep the bike upright was my only thought, but then the pain began to surge in waves of discomfort. Something had struck me. A bird? There was no one in front of me. I reached up, and the bike decelerated as I cupped my hand over my shoulder. Grit? It was gritty. I had been tagged by something hard. A rock? I supposed someone could have been standing in the grass median of a four-lane highway throwing gritty chunks of what felt like, could have been . . . cement? I stopped at the next gas station to find a round impact spot with a sunburst pattern of gray dust all around it. I topped off the tank gazing into the night sky. There was no moon, but stars by the millions.

Route 301 to 441, Marion County, I was close, just a few miles to go, but even those seemed to drag on into a never-ending night. Ocala, Belleview, I stopped to call my brother, I was sure I came too far. I hadn't. "Country miles," I finally understood it.

I arrived in Summerfield, a small hole in the wall just south of Ocala. My uncle lived on Lake Weir and was expecting me. I hadn't seen Uncle Don since I was a boy. He'd left early in the morning before we were awake, but the pile of loose change he left behind on the old wood stove eased my disappointment. It was the same wood stove I piled the scraps of my life on before I left: old bills, notices, demands, a restraining order, junk mail, and the *Easy Rider* magazine that started this whole tedious trek into the wilderness. I couldn't find the house, so I called. No one was home. I waited by the pay-phone in the parking lot of a Handy Way that had just closed for the night. They had been at a Christmas party.

We partied all week long. It was the best Christmas I could remember since finding out Santa Claus wasn't real. Jim Beam was the flavor of the house. I hadn't seen my cousin Aura Lee since she was a little girl. We smoked weed and caught up. I hooked up with another bag before the week was out. I was as ready as I could be for Daytona.

I raced through the Ocala National Forrest, found my way through Daytona, and at the intersection of Routes 92 and A1A—six stories of whitewashed stucco trimmed in Key West Blue. Across the street, a gas station, behind that, a tittie bar called the Shark Lounge. A1A ran north and south. Hotels, bars, souvenir stands, and fast food joints were crammed in as far as the eye could see—most were closed for the season making the place seem gray, inhospitable. Sand blew in off the beach, silently slithering over the empty streets like some kind of tourist-trap ghost town. The cropped beaches I'd seen in pictures looked warmer in magazines than they did in reality.

Finding the hotel bar on the way to check-in, I welcomed myself to Florida. The bartender was friendly with long dark hair thinning at the crown and a full beard. He bought me several shots of my first Jägermeister and drank a few himself. His sense of humor dripped with tired sarcasm. I thought that Daytona Beach was going to be a healthy place for new beginnings—how naive. I wasn't prepared for the reality of where I had landed.

I left the bar through the inside entrance. The lobby was to the right and was spacious, comfortably furnished, and upholstered in red. From where I came out of the bar, the front desk was across the lobby and to the right. To my left and down the hall were a gift shop and a couple vacant souvenir shops that were closed for the season. I saw the ocean through the glass of a restaurant, also closed. Above the front desk a disclaimer stated that occupants assumed their own risk in knowing the establishment wasn't equipped with a fire sprinkler system. I didn't think twice.

I leaned on my elbows and smiled. The clerk was my own age and friendly. She was from Maryland. I filled out a three-by-five index card with my name, address, vehicle-plate, and license number. She explained about the telephones and receiving mail. I wrote the hotel's address as my own. She took five hundred dollars for the first two months. My cash was running nervously low, but I was officially a resident of Florida.

I felt somewhat grounded again having checked in, but it could have been the Jäger. No one knew my story or the embarrassing failures I left behind. From here, I could be no better or no worse than anyone else.

A couple guys walked through, and the clerk flirted a little before she introduced them all as being "AMI guys."

I went outside through the bar, untied my things from the bike, and bought a round for the bartender and me on the way back through. I began to realize how laid back everyone seemed to be, and I began to consider making this alien place home.

I stepped off the elevator to the sixth floor. Walking down the long crimson-rug hallway for the first time, veiled women of Middle Eastern descent peered out of and quickly shut each door as I passed. Saddle bags hung from my left shoulder, duffle from the right. My army boots fell hard against the floor, and keys banged against my wallet chain swinging at my side, tapping in stride with every other step. No one seemed to come or go from these rooms, but keeping watch, the women were always there.

Opening the door to my room for the first time, the air seeped into the hallway, giving everything a musty hotel aroma. There was a bathroom to the right, tiled in yellow, old but clean. There was a kitchenette to the left with a full size refrigerator, stove, microwave, coffee pot, sink, and a decent amount of counter space. The carpet was crimson, the same color as the one I had been sleeping on in my parent's cellar. The back wall was draped with a curtain, except for the far right corner where there was a door leading outside. I laid my bags on the queen sized bed nearest the window, withdrew the curtain and had a view of the parking lot through a thick plate window that rose to the ceiling.

I opened the door and stepped onto the balcony; I had a decent view of the ocean. Porpoises were breaking the water's surface, swimming southward parallel to the beach. I felt dreadfully alone with only the wind carrying the muted sound of waves breaking on the surf. Below me, wisps of sand swirled through the parking lot. My motorcycle looked like a toy. Everything familiar was suddenly untouchable, and I began to wonder if I would ever return to Massachusetts.

I thought about my daughter and regretted the distance I'd placed between us—my only regret. Seaside stretched northward, and I had a clear view of A1A to where the city became a pin point on the horizon. Loneliness took me by surprise. There was nowhere to run if it all came crashing down. Overwhelmed, I just stood there in the salty breeze, and cried.

Part of the deal with the cheap room was that students of AMI were paired up as roommates, and mine arrived the next day. Doug was a baby-faced kid, eighteen, and raced rice rockets on the circuit. He was confident, almost cocky, and his parents were footing the bill—I don't think he was happy to meet his roommate.

I offered him a pull on a pint of Jim Beam, and he hit it hard taking almost half the bottle. Then he left the room abruptly, disappearing for a half-hour. I figured it was his first pull of the bourbon, and it got the better of him. I imagined he was puking over a railing somewhere. He returned, oddly enough, straight-faced. He had his room reassigned the next day.

Classes began, and I spent the first few days taking it all in and trying to follow a mouth-closed-ears-open approach. Everyone was strange, cautious, untrusting.

I settled into a routine that included a breakfast burrito at the school's snackateria, a diner-sized set up in the back corner of campus. The building was formally a resort-style compound rumored to belong to a mob boss at one time. An outer perimeter of buildings (once living suites) enclosed a large area with a central swimming pool. The story was that the swimming pool, which was also on the flight line of Daytona's International Airport, was used as a target for planes to drop packages.

About two weeks into classes I was trying to eat breakfast, leaning against the wall, waiting for a table to open.

"Hey, hey,"

I turned to look.

I said nothing but glanced in their direction. The younger of the two was looking right at me, gesturing for me to sit. He had straight black hair parted in the middle and a braid that hung just beyond the middle of his back. He was tall and thin, with something like a Fu Man-chu, and had thick-leather-gauntlets buckled around lean forearms. I recognized him as Kirk from class.

With a heavy North Carolina drawl, the older said, "Come on, have a seat." One of his eyes was offset and clouded, like from a head injury.

I was grateful and cautious. The older, although he spoke softly, looked every bit the part of hell on wheels. His inside forearm was tattooed with a side-by-side shotgun barrel and a Viking. His hair was long and braided; he was short, thick as a tree trunk. My first impression was that people didn't fuck with this man.

"Yea, sit down and eat man," Kirk said sliding in.

"Thanks," I said. "I'm Chris, I remember you're Kirk." I looked across the table at the grizzly guy. He held his hand out.

"James Huffman, proud to know you," he said, biting into a sandwich.

James and Kirk were from North and South Carolina respectively. James had been involved in a barroom gunfight between two clubs back home. Pleading the fifth, refusing to lie for one of his brothers, and also refusing to turn state's evidence he was more or less in Florida waiting for things to cool down.

I later learned there had been some bad blood over him not testifying. Kirk was a brother tagging along, a wingman. He had witnessed that the only shot James fired was a hole in the floorboard of his truck. Kirk never saw who pulled the trigger in the fight, but he saw enough to know it wasn't James. Both arrived in Daytona armed with revolvers and always seemed to be on alert.

Kirk and James roomed on the second floor at my hotel, right above the bar. They drove from South Carolina in a fifty-three Chevy pickup with Kirk's red ape-hung 48 pan-head in the back and everything else he owned (mostly tool boxes) bungee corded to the sides—á la Beverly Hillbillies.

James rode a shovel, FX rigid frame, dull silver. His cage was a Chevy Cavalier. He had a girlfriend in Winston Salem, and he was devoted to her. He and I began sitting together in class, and I noticed he had a hard time taking notes. He couldn't write as fast as the instructors spoke. He would trace over the first letter of each word as he had to think about what to write next. I'd take his notebook to keep him caught up with the lectures, filling in what he missed in the lag time where I finished writing before they were done speaking. James was a smart old mountain goat, but not in an academic context. He wasn't the sort of man who ever had a need to think as fast as the instructors were talking, which wasn't that fast. I came to know him as soft spoken and gentle.

Seaside living became more excitement than James could tolerate, said he couldn't get any studying done with all the partying that went on. He rented a trailer in a quiet park in New Smyrna. When he moved out, I moved down to the second floor with Kirk and "Momma," as she called herself. Melanie (her real name) was Kirk's pregnant girlfriend who found her way to Daytona to be with him.

I started drinking Miller High Life, a big leap for a Bud man. Miller was Kirk's brand, and it made beer runs simpler. Kirk didn't think much of Harley's Evo, which was what I was riding, but he was impressed that my stock 1200 could outrun his 96" stroker, and the fact that besides regular maintenance I rarely had to fix it. He was constantly fixing his pan head. Clutch baskets, primary cases, chains, and various parts and pieces of his bike tattooed their black oily outlines on our room's crimson carpet. We spent a good bit of time chasing down bike parts and push-starting his antique Chevy. I was more than happy to jump out and push whenever needed. Having a vehicle other than a motorcycle was a luxury, even if it meant having to move the windshield wipers manually before vacuum pressure could take over to run themselves. Whatever its quirks it was one vehicle more than I had.

Kirk and Momma argued a lot, and it got awkward at times, but we managed to maintain a good friendship. We were both strapped for cash.

Two months into school I was still out of a job. I had been able to borrow rent money from someone back home, but we were even more broke than that. One day, in desperation to find beer money, we moved all the washing machines in the laundry room to look for quarters. By the end of January I still hadn't found work, and we were eating wilted lettuce and catsup on stale bread. My girlfriend back home, (I was continuing a long distance phone-sex relationship with the girl from the Christmas party), was helping me out wherever she could, mailing me a carton of smokes and a few bucks once in a while.

Partying however was never a problem. It was easy to find someone in the hotel willing to share beer, and there were even two German guys on the third floor who went to AMI for watercraft mechanics. They threw joints down from their balcony every so often, and I thought it was the promised land. It rained joints! I went up there once. They were Nazi's and all they talked about was Hitler and drinking. I drank with them until I threw up all over the balcony, dark rum straight up.

Every day was about school and drinking. The two went hand in hand. A well-regulated regimen of partying and taking notes was effort enough to keep up a 3.7 GPA, and I liked what I was doing. I was good with a wrench. Not that school was all about spinning wrenches, it wasn't. There was just as much mechanical theory and mathematics involved. We spent several weeks in the classroom before even picking up a wrench. James would get pissed because he'd study his ass off to do well, and I'd do just as well with a hangover.

Lunch breaks were all about the pub. There was a group of guys who were regulars at JJ's Pub, a barroom a few miles down the road. They had cheap lunch deals for AMI guys. If I had a couple dollars I could get a sandwich or a couple beers, but the beer I found tasted so much better when I had only enough money for one or the other.

As the tourist season approached I was able to find a job through a local I'd met at the hotel bar. He had a friend who managed a restaurant, and he cautiously recommended me. Locals were used to seeing people like me come and go. People passing through were not known for being trustworthy, but I finally landed a job cooking nights and weekend days at Sophie Kay's Coffee Tree, a family restaurant in Ormond Beach north of Daytona on A1A. It was a decent job that paid the bills and kept me in cigarettes and beer. I'd switched to smoking Camels because they offered the third pack free and a T-shirt too.

Around the same time, a trailer became available in the park where James was staying, so Kirk and Momma moved out. I was glad to be by myself again. Momma's constant whining was annoying. Without another

AMI class scheduled to begin until after I graduated, there wouldn't be another roommate.

The real party starts in Daytona when Race Week and the 500 rolls up in March, from there the city becomes a summer-long cluster fuck of party animals. Bike Week follows. Or perhaps it's French Canadian Spring Break, which might come just before Race Week. There's even a separate Black Reunion Spring Break and a Gay Spring Break.

Getting to work on time through all the traffic became almost impossible. Bike Week arrived, and I wasn't ready for the magnitude of it all. I was scheduled to work with Team Harley-Davidson at the races, but somehow never made it there. My girlfriend flew to Tampa under the guise of a visit to her mother, and then she flew a puddle-jumper to Daytona.

It was surreal the way Bike Week crept in, like the city was Athens, and Zeus himself were coming to walk among the mortals. Everyone was looking forward to the "bikers" rolling in. Race Week was okay—not a lot of return for all the traffic jams and red-necks it brought. Spring Break was just a big party and a lot of mess for the trouble it brought. But the "bikers" spent money, and Bike Week marked the height of prosperity in the tourist season.

I once saw a t-shirt hanging in a Bike Week souvenir stand that summed it up nicely. It started with something like . . . *I don't smoke dope, chew rope* . . . and ended with . . . *And I've seen goats fuck in the marketplace, but I never seen anything like the shit that goes on here.* It was a lot to squeeze onto a t-shirt.

Morning light leaked in around the blinds, bathing the room in a dim maroon silence. I fumbled over the nightstand for the alarm clock and shook what was left of the previous night's barroom noise out of my head. I was still in my clothes, but it didn't matter, as there was no one to impress. It was March, Saint Patrick's Day, I stepped happily onto my balcony overlooking the bar's entrance. With only 10 weeks left of school I was half way there. Bike-Week had been over for three days, and I was still going strong.

I was comfortable with the home I was making for myself. I knew a few people, had money coming in, and my room was cheap. I was lucky because even though there wasn't another roommate, my rent remained at two-fifty. When I wasn't working or going to school, I was busy collecting stickers for my helmet from every biker bar in Volusia County: Froggies, Last Resort, Cabbage Patch, The Boot. I hit them all. I knew a couple people well enough to call them friends, and had earned the trust of a couple locals. My life had fallen into something that resembled normalcy.

It was a beautiful morning. Just a few lingering clouds hung over the beach, soon to be evaporated in the morning sun. I took in a lungful of the salted air while extracting a Camel Light from my black-leather-studded case that hung purposefully from my belt. Porpoises played on the high tide surf while I smoked and organized the upcoming day in my head—school all day, work from six to ten, maybe a few beers before bed—I was glad I had that straight. There was nothing else to worry about. I buckled the leather my girlfriend bought for me when she came for Bike Week. I was in love.

Fifteen minutes later I was in the parking lot warming up the bike. Each morning was a brand new indulgence, marveling at the sound of my exhaust banging back and forth between the hotel buildings. I listened to the combustion as the air-cooled cylinders began to warm. Valves made a pwhoping sound as the cam whirred with each twist of the throttle. I listened for any indication that maintenance was needed. I ran up the RPMs as I rolled out, in hopes of turning someone's hang-over into a nightmare. Every morning I wound it up just to make sure everyone was awake.

The air was refreshing, and the baffling crack of my pipes kept me in tune to the road. I rode with all seriousness, as if riding was the one defining activity of importance in the day. To top it off, I realized it was payday.

Occasionally I'd run into others making their way to school westbound on Route 92, and this morning was no different. I took up behind a pack of crotch rockets buzzing like angry mosquitoes. Light to light we sprinted past the hospital and the mall. Fast food joints blurred by at suicidal rates of speed, and a seven-thirty-seven coming in low overpowered our noise—the whole pack slowed, looking up at its metallic underbelly as it passed overhead. Daytona International Speedway marked the final mile. I hadn't passed anyone, but didn't let them get away from me either. Parking our machines, we proudly grinned at each other. High on adrenaline, we recalled the finer moments of the ride as we walked to the snacketeria. Mine was shooting out of a red light and laying the bike into a sideways skid to avoid someone on a bicycle. I guess he misjudged how fast I was going before stepping off the curb. I looked into his fright ridden face and his expression changed slightly. I thought he shit himself.

An eight o'clock lecture, 8:45 skill lab, back to lecture at 11, then lunch. The morning had progressed as beautifully as it had started. By noontime my bike was calling me. I asked a friend if he wanted to ride to JJ's Pub. Short on funds he declined. JJ's was a few miles further west where Daytona Beach turned rural. My bike had spent the morning on the Dynamometer, a nine hundred pound drum the motorcycle rides on to determine where horse power is lost and can be gained. I'd re-jetted the carb and was anxious to test out the improvements. The computer mock up of the horse power gain showed the new configuration beating the old in a simulated race. I was stoked for the ride. As the pipes warmed I zipped down my sleeves, pulled the cuffs of my gloves over my forearms, put on my favorite leather cap, and buckled a turtle shell over it. It was almost too warm to be wrapped in leather, but better safe than sorry.

Route 92 is one of those roads where the speed limit of 55 is a joke. 65 MPH is the average on any given day. As JJ's Pub came into view I backed off the throttle and began down shifting. I recognized some of the bikes parked out front. Andy, Russ, and some of the guys were already there. Approaching the entrance, I braked even harder to make the tricky right turn into the pub's sandy parking lot. It was a hazard pulling into the sand squarely so that the tires didn't slide from under but fast enough that I didn't leave my ass hanging in the road.

Inside the pub John heard something outside that sounded vaguely familiar and turned toward the door.

"What the hell was that?"

Brenda, the bartender, was serving up sandwiches; she looked out the side door at a large cloud of dust swirling in the air. She popped the top of a soda can and placed it in front of John.

"Oh my god, something happened out there, all the cars are stopping," she gasped as John drank from the can. Russ got up and walked to the door. An eighteen wheeler was pulled off to the side of the road about five hundred feet away. A small black car was parked behind it. The truck driver and the car's driver (an off duty Sheriff's deputy) appeared from around the front of the cab. They back-tracked toward the bar, searching along the tree line.

Everyone in the bar spilled into the parking lot. Brenda yelled inside. "JJ, call the police!"

The crowd watched as the two men turned back toward the truck, walked along its length from front to back, they bent over to look under the passenger side fuel tank, and appeared to be concerned with the gas tank. Russ ran down from the bar to see what was up.

The deputy called out to a lifeless foot shadowed by the tank. He was sure I was dead. "Hey, buddy?"

"Uh . . . Yea"

The truck driver grabbed his chest and fell to the ground.

John walked toward the truck with Andy right behind him. Russ ran out into the street and picked something up.

"It's Chris Christie's hat," he shouted.

John ran back to the bar, "Call the school," he screamed, "It's one of our guys!"

Sirens drew closer, and a police vehicle arrived.

"Where am I?"

"I'm going to be honest with you sir, you're under a truck."

"You've got to be fucking kidding me!" *A pick-up truck? I wasn't under a truck a moment ago, was I? I better crawl out of here.*

Emergency crews set up the Jaws of Life to remove the boarding ladder between me and the rescue effort. A bystander, a plumber with a hacksaw, was able to cut through it faster than the jaws could be assembled.

"Don't move Chris!"

"That's all right, I can crawl out myself."

I tried to lift my body with my arms, but only the left arm pushed against the ground. Why can't I move my right arm? Turning my head was difficult, but I managed to look right. My forearm was snapped like a pencil, my hand lying next to my elbow, and I was covered in blood.

Familiar voices were telling me not to worry, that I was going to be all right. Someone was telling someone else to just keep talking to me. Something was burning my leg, and there was something warm and thick running into my eye.

Don't cut my leather

My jeans were being cut away from my body. I could hear the material severing against the blades, I knew what that meant. Blackness.

"Chris!"

"Yeah." *Where am I?*

"We were able to save the vest, I only cut the laces," a faceless voice said. I felt a dim hint of satisfaction. Euphoria. Blackness.

The guys from the bar looked on as officers diverted traffic and marked the locations of things in the road: the bike, the seat, my glasses, a glove. Blood trailed down the street following the truck's path.

Where is my bike? What happened to the bike? "My Bike?"

"Don't worry, the bike is fine, the police will make sure no one touches it," came the faceless voice. Again, his words were reassuring.

I heard Kirk's voice. "You hang in there bro, we're all right here man."

"Chris, it's Russ. They're takin' good care of you."

"Chris, it's Jim Watts. We're all right here for you buddy," said the school's president. *What was all the fuss about?*

E. M. T s worked masterfully within the tight space as an exposed femoral artery pulsed with my heartbeat. Antifreeze drained from where my body impacted the truck's grill and burned into the road rash on my ankle. Critical care was taken to extract me, and I was carried into the ambulance in a geometrically contorted position on the stretcher. My left femur was snapped and had torn through the back of my thigh, tearing the skin from the bottom of my ass to the middle of the inside of my calf. Most of it, along with the muscle it protected, was grated into the road. My sciatic nerve was visible and damaged, and my femoral artery was draped across one of the jagged ends of femur protruding from my leg. If it let go, I would have bled out. A Med-Evac Chopper circled twice and landed, standing by just in case.

"Where am I?"

My eyes adjusted to the light.

"You're in the Halifax Medical Center in Daytona Beach," a woman's voice answered.

Delirious, disoriented slowly my eyes focused. The light was blinding. My voice barely audible.

Oh . . . that's . . . good.

I saw myself lying on the stretcher in front of something that resembled an oven door.

This is weird. "Why did they leave me . . . the oven . . . why am I in a kitchen?"

I have no recollection of where that conversation took place in relation to my arrival at Halifax Medical, but it stands out as my first memory from inside the hospital. It could have been in the first critical moments laid out on a triage stretcher, or at any other point during my first few weeks amid the numerous surgeries I required. Hind sighted, I often wonder if there are aspects of such situations so alarmingly horrible that their details are kept from patients. When I recall that particular waking memory, I wonder if I had regained consciousness in a morgue, as the images in my memory of the surroundings suggest to me. But then too, nothing was as it seemed.

I was initially admitted by Dr. Jose Dimayuga. Among others, Dr. James Acker was called in to consult on the multiple orthopedic injuries. He took responsibility for saving my leg when the general consensus was to amputate. All my wounds were grossly contaminated with ground in dirt, grime, and grass. Several surgical procedures for debridement were performed before any bones could be set. A hole was reamed down the length of the femur using a series of awls that ended with a 14mm. A 13 mm rush rod was inserted. Traction pins were placed below the femur and the knee. The leg was hung. An open-reduction-internal-fixation on the right radius and ulna was done—a five-hole-semi-tubular-plate secured with five 3.5mm screws and a 20mm screw. A rush rod was hammered into my humerus to keep the proximal fragment of the bone in proper alignment. Multiple full-thickness wounds covered my legs, and superficial cuts, abrasions, and bruises were everywhere. Antibiotics were added to my IV regimen: Rocephin, Ancef, Gentamicin, Penicillin, Timentin, and Tobramycin. My body was under microbe attack from organisms native to the Bayou region of Louisiana. I had not a high probability of surviving the first night, and if I did, infections were doing their best to finish the job. I was assessed at risk of alcohol withdrawal, and Librium was added to the cocktail.

There is a trapeze looming over my head. I cannot reach out to grab it, however I strain to try. Machines surround me, lights flash, monitors glow and beep, and wires and tubes umbilical me to them. My head is pounding, legs immobile—pounding, my arms—pounding. Room fades to black. No sound except inert mumbling voices. People mill about in a vaguely familiar and smoky bar room, ugly-mug faces I think I know but can't be sure in the dim unsettled light, I hear my unspoken name.

"Sir."

As if being sucked by a giant vacuum nozzle the smoke clears and the trapeze bar materializes again. A man with a white coat and clipboard stands over me. He takes my pulse and motions to a woman in blue at the foot of the bed.

"What? Where am I?" I manage to groan, and the effort takes all my strength.

"We're going to insert a catheter," he callously replies, as though the news is supposed to be the highlight of my day. A sinking feeling overtakes me. A tear rolls over my cheek, and the room goes black.

I'm in a large cylindrical tank. Glossy walls surround me. They are wrinkled and dripping wet like a freshly drained pool—puddles on the floor, and everything is the same sleek shade of blue. I am standing in the center of this tank as something thicker than water slowly drips, drips, and . . . . drips. Every heavy drop strikes the floor and echoes in my ears, and I can see myself standing there, I am looking in from a glass window high above, arms out, neck arched back, helpless to escape, like on the cover of a paper-back I once read. A naked man strung from wires, *Coma*. The echoing drip surrounds me.

In the distance, a man holds what appears to be a neck collar. "You've broken your cervical spine," His face contorts and sags as he hovers over, securing the device around my neck. I'm amused by music in the background and ask him to turn it up, but there is none playing. I ask him for a mirror and for the first time I look myself in the eye. My hair is matted with dried blood. Facial wounds, thickly scabbed over, grotesquely stand out. It was not me.

"My name is Dr. Slade. I'm you're plastic surgeon. I did a pretty good job reattaching your ears." He tried to sound positive. "The avulsions should be unnoticeable."

The ear lacerations consisted on the left side of avulsion of most of the posterior skin covering the cartilage. This was an avulsion in the area where one would commonly take a full-thickness skin graft off the posterior skin. The cartilage was completely exposed in this area and the edges were ragged.

On the right side, the helix was split; this was split from the anterior attachment of the helix, down across the antihelical fold into the concha. The cartilage was very frayed and macerated as were the skin edges.

I can hear "The Price Is Right" but cannot see a television. It must be daytime. My glasses are a twisted scrap of metal, one lens gone and the other deeply gouged. There is a pair that is not mine, but I cannot wear them. They make me dizzy; everything looks zig-zagged, warped, as it might in the background of a fun house mirror.

I am in hell.

Somehow I convince myself I'll be on my feet again in just two weeks. Two more weeks and I'll go on with my life, catch up on the schoolwork I'm missing, and pick up where left off. I wonder what repairs my Harley might need.

Two weeks come and go, but I learn there was a two-week period *before* what I thought were these first two. Two weeks that even now are only sparse nonlinear images of what I'm able to remember. The severity of my situation reveals itself: visits from doctors, painful prodding at my wounds, endless morphine trips, new obstacles every day. Each awakening slaps me in the face with another grim version of reality, and then I slip off into the deepest caverns of my mind.

"Where am I?"

My eyes refuse to focus through the tunnel vision. I have no sense of time or sensation of being. A woman stands over me.

"Where am I"

"You're at the Halifax Medical Center in Daytona Beach."

ROADKILL

"Oh, "
I return to delirium.

I'm confused, disoriented, crying. I tell myself I'll be on my feet soon enough. God! What am I going to have to catch up on at school? Every day is an alien autopsied nightmare of morphine trips and surgery, where faceless Grays stand over me. I loose consciousness under the knife every day. In just two more weeks I will shed this choking bola of surgical tubing, that forces the cold, green, irritating smell of oxygen down my throat. Rip this needle from my vein that I may feed myself by my own hand, the only one I have, and wash my blood caked hair. Each day is lost in the next, two weeks pass me by, my spirit not yet broken, because there are still two more.

My job. Oh my god, my job! I hope someone can cover my shifts. I hope they don't think I pulled a no-call-no-show. I hope they still have a job for me when I get out of here in a couple weeks.

I can't feel the tears trailing my cheek, but they are cold and wet as they run inside my ears at the foot of a grassy hill. Joyous people are partying all around me, calliope music fills the air. There is a brightly lit and festively decorated house on top of the hill with a large farmer's porch. People are having a great celebration, and I want to join them. I climb the hill toward the house, and a funny little man, perhaps a leprechaun, is wearing green hair and bright pink trousers. He dances a jig in front of me, mocking. I don't make it to the house on the hill.

A presence looms over me. My eyes focus. I barely remember where I am. I reach for my morphine button and administer a shot. A uniformed state trooper wearing latex gloves and holding a clipboard stands elongated in the slanted doorway.
"Hello, how are you feeling?"
"How does it look?"
He doesn't say anything.
"That bad then?" I try to make light of things.
"You did alright," he says, stepping forward. "I have to ask you sir, are there any details about the accident you can remember, anything at all?
The last thing I remember is the sound of the bike's engine racing, climbing in pitch as the rpms suddenly spiked. My hand, gloved tightly in leather was wrenched from the throttle when the back wheel was force-locked between the pavement and the massive chrome bumper of a cab-over Kenworth traveling at roughly 60 MPH.

I visualize my body as my back hit its grill squarely, my arms cocked outward and legs still crooked at the knee as though in the saddle. Next thing, a strange sensation, like sitting on a roller coaster high at the top of a hill, and when the car finally drops, there is that moment of free fall, a tickling spin deep in the gut that ends in the throat with the heart skipping a beat—something had taken me out of myself. Looking down on the scene below, everyone moved in slow motion. There was no sound, not even the dim shush of blood flowing through idle eardrums. The light, I traveled through it, warping, and back again—I touched the universe for what could have been seconds on earth—or years.

"I've been told not to say anything about the accident one way or the other. They got me on some pretty good dope and I don't know what I'm saying half the time."

My diatribe sounds rehearsed. I smile inside as I realize I'm fucked up on drugs in the presence of a cop. "My lawyer's card is on the table, you can call him with any questions," I continued. How did I know to say any of that?

"Thank you for your time Mr. Christie."

Rick Tresher, my attorney, must be the reason for how I answered the trooper. I find a representation agreement on my bedside table. It was signed on the 22nd, five days after I was admitted, five days for which I have no sense of time.

Rick's Tresher's assistant Kim stands in the doorway holding up a new pair of glasses. "The optometrist was able to gage your prescription from one of the broken lenses"

I can see beyond the call button, beyond the overhead rigging, and into the shadowy crannies of a pock-specked drop ceiling. A small wall mounted television dangling on a tiny platform at the end of a mechanical arm. I see the screens of my monitors, and the faces on the heads of everyone who walks past my glass-bound room. I'm a spectacle, a specimen, on display like a great medical freak of nature.

My morphine pump beeps to indicate a dose is administered, and the fuzzy melting image of a nurse is standing over me.

"I can do my own morphine. I don't need anyone to do it for me".

She hangs two different bags on the IV tree. I'm pissed off at her for shooting me up while I was unconscious and more so for my own helplessness.

"What are those?"

"Those are your nutrients." She tries to be delicate with her words.

I'm being fed through a tube? I flash to the "tube feeders" at the nursing homes I worked. I feel dizzy, sick, blackout.

Rick Tresher stands over my bed. "You ain't one of those guys I see on TV, are you?"

"No, I do not advertise on television," he chuckles.

"Good, then there's still hope for me!" It is good to see him. Hope.

A beautiful girl stands at the foot of the bed, cursing under her breath, and another enters the room.

"You need a hand?"

"The damn catheter bag just spilled all over the bed." The stench of urine fills the room.

I don't think they know I am awake, so I just lay silently, wallowing in humiliation. They leave the room and return with four other people. Five of them gently lift me off the bed. I can see my feet. Bandages cover my legs, both of them, all the way up, and there are wires everywhere. I'm looking at a traction rig and try my hardest to keep my wits about me as the sixth person, the girl who was first in the room, changes the bedding beneath me.

"I like the view from up here." The nurse holding up my left shoulder is providing me with a clear shot down her blouse. "No bra!"

"Oh great, now he's going to spill the catheter every day." She smiles at me.

The room erupts in laughter and I laugh even though my ribs are busting and the wounds on my face begin to stretch and sting. I realize laughter and pain will have to coexist inside me if I want laughter at my bedside. With one moment of humility I learn of its magic. I deploy it as a tactic, a wall, something to hide behind.

I start using a sense of humor to diffuse uncertainty, humiliation, and mostly to give back a moment of lightness to those burdened so heavily with my care. I live with the knowledge that I am a man on the edge. I might soon become to any of them the patient no one wants to loose.

But how do I begin to laugh when the doctor's words come so coldly? He prods and bends my injuries to the point of white-flashing pain.

"I have to be up front with you."

My wrist bends unwillingly in his grip. I can feel the metal, the screws inside in my bones. They don't bend and eventually give. They snap sudden, violent.

"It's unlikely you'll get out of bed again."

I become a shell. I think about running, my daughter. Everything I'll never do rushes me at once. All I've lost slaps me in the face like the doctor standing there indifferently, blunt, no misconceptions.

His candor is appreciated, and I briefly go numb.

I fight to keep my courage on the surface. The doctor leaves, and the nurse check the IV pumps. She leaves. I explode.

For what have I given my right arm, retracted, atrophic, and these four sterile walls that beset me? I must withdraw so deeply within myself. How to escape their tormenting stare? Just once more to walk and touch their flat-satin gaze. May they cease to encumber me and set me free. But my world is confined to the pressing of buttons, and the only feeling left in my heart is the returning pain. Please merciful button, let me soar outside these walls inside myself.

My daughter's favorite toy was a white and pink Big-Wheel. She always brought it with her on our weekends together. Tiny pebbles of asphalt crunch and grind against the road as she rolls along. Blonde, her baby-fine hair swings in time with her shoulders, looking back to make sure I am keeping up as her legs crank on the pedals. My own voice taunts me with despair—sorry honey, daddy can't walk you home today.

There is nothing anywhere. No sound, no walls, no machines. I am alert and aware of myself. There is no mattress below me, the overhead is gone. No needle secured by tape protrudes from back of my hand. A woman materializes, taking form before my eyes—a creeping mist. She hovers over me, her body at arms length. Her hair gold and flowing, and I lock into her eyes. She smiles down on me, and I have a great sense of safety.

Her arms are wide, welcoming, draped with smooth flowing sleeves, long and drifting as though aloft on the same currents that hold her hair from falling—like floating under water in a gentle flowing river. We look into each others eyes. I never want this to end, and she remains silent, but her voice is alive inside me, a feeling of love and well-being.

Her hands reach for my face, nearly touching it as she drifts away. She fades into the mist or becomes the mist itself. I try to rise, to follow. I need to feel her touch. She fades further away—her reassuring finger tips.

Monitors beep, tubes and wires strangle, and I slip out from under their hold as the noise coming from the bank of instruments at my head indicates that my oxygen levels are dangerously low. Two nurses rush to my side and begin refitting the tubing to my face. I smile dreamily.

My little brother Don stands on his toes trying to pull down the frozen press blankets our father brought home from work to shield the wood pile. I retrieve the wheelbarrow and a hand-truck from the shed and set them in the snow. Side by side with my brother we free the stiff cracking rubber covers. They fall, and a foot of snow showers the top of our heads and melts inside the necks of our unzipped snorkels. He kicks at the ice still caked to them as I drag the mats to the side. Grudgingly, he lays logs across the hand-truck, and I throw them in the wheelbarrow. Our noses freeze inside, and I wheeze white puffs of breath in the crisp dry air—fog freezes to my glasses, I fish my inhaler out of my pocket, and pull in two deep breaths. My heart races for a second, then I breathe easier. We stack the wood almost heavier than we can handle to avoid making a second trip.

Don and I groan to each other about the chore, struggling to make headway toward the house over a poorly shoveled uphill path.

I hear my Grandmother's voice. "If you just bring in a few at a time when you come home from school or when you come in from playing every day it wouldn't be such a chore."

It makes perfect sense to me now that my gloves are soaked and my fingers numb from picking up logs that toppled into the snow as the wheelbarrow capsized.

It is autumn, and I am enamored with the smells of russet and gold and hues of ocher splashed with crimson. My father cuts down a tree. I ride beside him in the dump truck he built for hauling wood, a one-ton International. He tells me things a boy needs to know—chainsaws, oil, and how much wood is in a cord. We are in a store renting a log splitter.

The man behind the counter has no face, only wildly tangled whiskers, and I turn my head, afraid, and find myself standing beside my brother again. This time we are building stacks of wood. My father appears, angry at the unsatisfactory job we've done and knocks it all down.

My brother strips his wet clothes by the fire as I watch from outside the window, freezing. I cannot find my way back inside.

I awake shivering, cold, the familiar sights and sounds of my room again surrounding me—the IV pump growls, and I long to be home among the pine groves where I ran as a boy. I ran . . . . I ran . . . . I try not to think about running and remember trudging through the forest knee deep in snow. The pines are heavily laden—their branches bow before me, and nothing of the world can find me except the low moan of wind and the bass-rich-plop as clumps of ice and snow release themselves from the branches to the beckoning ground. My cold cramped legs drive on, and I jump in start of the brittle snap-crack—frozen breaking limbs.

My heart is racing as a shadow appears in the doorway against the backlight of the hallway, and I roll my head in the opposite direction. I'm not talking to anyone today. It's a bad day. The familiar voice of my younger brother calling crawls inside my head. "Duuuuude."

I almost think it's my imagination, I can't tell the difference anymore, but Don is actually standing before me and I am elated. The face of my brother brings color to my cheeks, and he shows me his speeding ticket—104 mph in North Carolina. He made it from Massachusetts to Daytona in less than a day.

Don fills me in on news from home. Two days after I crashed, Ma got a phone call from the hospital wanting to know if she was aware that her son was in an accident. "Of course," she said. "Wait a minute? Which one?" Our little brother Adam, seventeen years old, also went down in a motorcycle accident. He was okay, though.

"Chris . . . Chris . . . ?"
I hear my name like someone has their head stuck in a tin-can.
"Your brothers are here."
The nurse pushes the button to raise my head. My rib cage stresses to the breaking point, I breathe slowly to adjust to the elevation. Everything comes into view, and I am smiling, high, still enjoying wherever I was when they pulled me from my nap. She leaves the room and James and Kirk come in. Brothers—I get it. James is laughing.

"Those nurses wanted to know how many brothers you have," he said. I'm happy to see him. I feel safe in his presence. The smell of leather cuts through the smell of bandages and whiteness. I am safe.

"Hey bro," Kirk starts with his SC drawl. "You are the toughest mother fucker I've ever met. Man they pulled you from under that truck and you were ready to kick somebody's ass! Man, that truck driver is probably still scared."

Kirk puts his hand on my shoulder.

"They have your bike over at the school and nobody is going to touch it. It's locked up," James says.

"Hey man, Brenda at JJ's is getting a poker run together for you. You know, try to raise a little money to help you out and all," Kirk jumps in.

"Yea, we'll all be ridin' for you bro," James adds.

The news is great even if I can't show as much enthusiasm. James says a bunch of guys had been over to see me, but that I was out cold all the time. I had faint memories of faces. They all said they were my brother; it was the only way the hospital would let them into the CCU. Gold-Wing, (so named because he was in love with his Gold-Wing) was the owner of the mysterious glasses on the bedside table. James says that he had them laying around as an extra pair and brought them by hoping they would help. I recall Gold Wing being there—just barely.

Days later. James comes by for another visit. My mother walks in the room. She looks at him uncomfortably. She says the day before she had seen him across from her as she was talking to some people from the school and her first thought was she'd hate to run into him in a dark alley. He scared her from behind his red wrap around shades.

Her eyes begin to well. I muster every bit of strength I can find. "Don't even think about balling your eyes out, Ma!" She bursts into a half laughing, half crying smile. James introduces himself and leaves the room.

"I feel so much better now that I've heard you speak. You sound a lot better than you look," Ma says. Her tears eventually stop.

It's the next day, and James is here again. Ma seems okay with him now. They conspire with the nurses to start me eating solid food, and James holds a Whopper to my face so I can eat. They knew that all I've been thinking about lately is a milkshake. I probably mentioned it to James once or twice, or maybe the nurses heard me talking in my sleep. An orgasm of strawberry-chilled-melty-goodness—the scars on my face fracture sucking paradise through a straw.

My poker run is today. I wish I were in the wind. Will I ever ride again? The day drags by. They all drag namelessly past me. Ma stops in at the end of the day to say goodbye. She and the uncles stopped by JJ's. I wish I could have been there to see the look on her face when she saw the couple fucking on a picnic table. To hear her tell it is priceless enough.

She leaves as she came, with tears. "I'm glad you have that rough-tough cream puff looking out for you." she weeps.

"He is an angel—I'll see ya Ma."

"I'm sorry your dad couldn't make it"

"Didn't expect him to Ma. I'll see ya Ma."

Rick Tresher was busy in the outside world getting to the bottom of my predicament, and he keeps me posted. I see him or his assistant Kim regularly. The case would be closed if not for one simple thing. The truck driver has three different stories as to what exactly happened. When he first stepped out of the truck there was an off-duty deputy already on the scene. The driver's first words were, "I didn't even see him." Then he told the state police that I was flying in the left lane and cut him off into the right lane. This doesn't wash because the off-duty deputy said that if I was going *that* fast to turn into *that* pub from the left lane, then I would have had to been passing his car at an excessive rate of speed. That didn't happen. He also gave a third statement to the local news crew. Forensic reconstructionists review photos of the scene. Rick places flyers in all the local convenience stores calling for anyone who may have witnessed the impact or anything at all as I was being dragged down the road. Unbelievable that on a busy highway like route 92 nobody saw anything.

Finally, my condition stabilized and I am moved from the ICU to a room on the ninth floor, room 910 on the cardio care unit. It is the only ward with a private room available to accommodate my isolation precaution order. I was still considered a contamination risk for whatever microbe is still infecting me, and for the risk that I also have in becoming infected. My wounds are still open. I'm still at the mercy of fate.

They have me pumped full of antibiotics, the high-octane variety, Rocephin and Vancomyacin. They're shooting Heparin into me daily, a blood thinner injected into the soft flesh around my naval. It is becoming tracked and tender. At first the shots were annoying, now they are painful.

However beneficial, my daily cocktail regimen is not without its lack of side effects. It has been weeks since I've moved my bowels, and I'm not quite sure if I ever will again. It was made clear to me (during one of those half conscious-conversations somewhere in the past weeks) that there's a certain amount of constipation to be expected, a sort of side effect of the meds that drip down the surgical tubing, through the growling pumps, and into my viens. If I can accomplish this one simple bodily function, overcome this hurdle, it will serve as a sign of wellness; with all that remains broken inside myself, to be able to go to the bathroom seems like a logical way to start getting on with life, something I can work on. There will be a sense of progress with the intestines doing their job as prescribed, but therein sits a problem.

Secretly, I suspect it is more of what I have to go through to take a dump that was keeping me from taking it, however much I look foreword to making that move. I'm shy by nature, not like people I have known who find it a normal course of action to sit on a throne, or stand at a urinal and carry on a conversation with no shame whatsoever. Mounted on top of dignity, other obstacles make the ordeal daunting.

First there's this cold hard pan that they expect me to sit on, which is fine, only I'm completely incapable of maneuvering my body into a sitting position. And then there's the issue of the depth of the pan. There couldn't have been more than three inches between the rim and its bottom. I was sure that wouldn't do; there is nowhere for the mess to disperse itself but up. I dread the moment, the moment when I ring the nurses' station and have to ask for assistance. It's inevitable, no way to avoid it. I pass time trying to think of the best way to make the request.

Fearing the worst (which was when the problem would become an enema candidate), I practice hoisting myself off the mattress with my left arm. My right arm is retracted, atrophic, and the hand curled under, closed in a fist that I can't open. It is difficult to raise myself without my body falling to the right. Surges of pain rush up and down my legs with every attempt I make to raise myself, but soon I am able to "chin-up" to the trapeze bar. It feels good, the surge of blood in my arm, useful for something again. Moving in such a way worked the weakening muscles in my neck, my face. There too it is good to feel the sensation of blood flow, a small victory in realizing that I'm not such a fixture to the mattress.

It's progress, but it isn't enough that I can hoist myself off the pillow. I still have to figure out how to lift my pelvis and hold myself long enough to cram a foot-long turd into a three-inch pan. After a while I figure it all out. I just have to wait for the moment and do it.

I am finally ready; nature's calling rang in during the evening shift. Evening staff was not scheduled consistently, so there is a good chance that the nurse attending me will be someone I don't have to face on a regular basis. Unfortunately it is one of the regular girls, but by the time I'm ready for the bedpan I don't care anymore. I just want to get it over with. I repress the embarrassment and chuckle nervously about it, trying to make light of the unpleasant situation.

It drains my pride when the nurse watches me lift my body off the mattress, pity written all over her face. Humility takes a whole new perspective as she makes sure my gown is properly opened in the back. I feel like an animal, or a child, helpless and on display, something to be the subject of conversation, even if only to her husband or the lady who works the cash register in the cafeteria.

It's easy to hold myself in position at first; I'd been practicing for a few days. I hold my chin up tight to the bar and roll my hips forward and to the side as best I can while she slides the chilly steel pan under my ass.

I feel the blood vessels filling in my face as I tell the nurse that I will be fine, I'll call her when I'm finished. She is still in the room when I push for the first time. It's hard to hang there, and I can't wait.

Pain surges through my body like a hammer pounding simultaneously everywhere that was broken inside me. I could feel the catheter inside me, more annoying than ever. Her face contorted like it hurt her as well. She steps forward, placing an arm beneath my shoulder to help hold me up. "I can do it," I said, "Please go." She leaves as a surge of emotion runs through me and I start to cry. I push again, hard, from the diaphragm, but received no reward.

The arm holding me in the air cramps at the elbow, and I grab the trapeze even tighter, curling my wrist to gain some leverage. Again I strain to tighten every muscle in my lower torso, and my entire body breaks out in a sweat as the first sensation of movement comes right at the end of the push. I exhaled and try to relax. My fingers go numb as I clench up for another try.

Finally, some progress. I am defecating. I grip the bar tighter, fighting to stay up as the bulk tries to find room to expand in the shallow pan. My grip let go and I fall on the bed. Waves of heat surge through my limbs. My head pounds. I lay uncomfortably on top of the pan, angry with myself for not being able to finish. I manage to lift myself again, and in another grueling effort I finish making the mess.

I call the nurse who comes in with an aide. They rolled me on my side and my mind goes numb. I sink below melancholy as the young girl goes about the business of wiping my ass.

I become dreadfully aware of my limitations. With this one simple task of every day existence so far out of my grasp, I dwell on things I think I will never touch again: walking, running, freedom, independence. So many things seem impossibly far away.

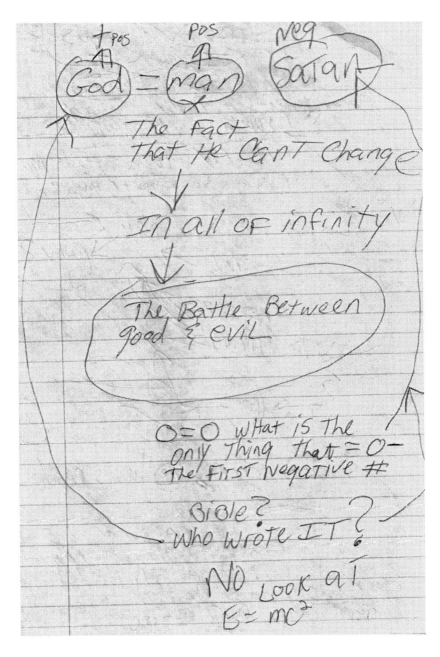

A notebook excerpt from a moment of madness.

Original Manuscript

View approaching JJ's Saloon

Points of Impact

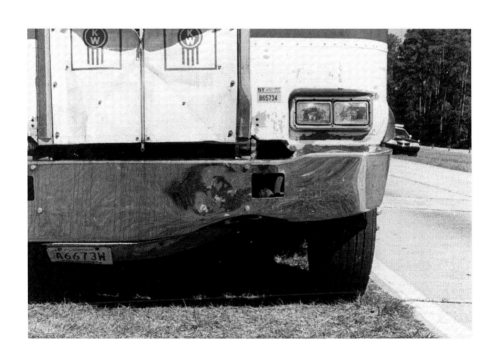

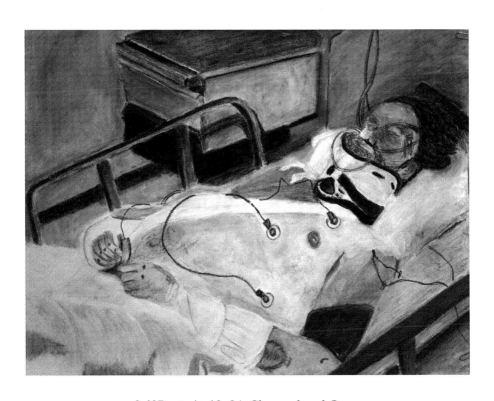

Self Portrait: 18x24, Charcoal and Gesso

1990 Harley Davidson XLH 1200
Rest in Peace

Cartoon Network drowns ambient noises from the hallway as I lay here. Where the fuck else am I going with a leg propped up in a frame? How am I going to go about getting my atrophic hand to open? I cram a tube of toothpaste inside my curled over fingers. Pain nails my head to the pillow, but I swallow it. The tube presses into my palm, my fingers resist, nerves tell the hand to fist, but the fingers remain still. My wrist knots up; the nerves end here.

It seems unfair that a man holding a CDL endorsed for Haz-Mat, double, and triple trailers has also been (on separate instances) charged with reckless driving, leaving the scene, DUI, operating without a license, failure to identify accountability for property damage, two different instances of speeding one with regard to a commercial vehicle, and failure to pay a fine. All this is only from the past seven year block of the 48-year-old trucker's life.

I answer the phone and a man's voice shyly speaks up.

"Uh, yea, uh, is this the young guy that was hit by the truck out on 92?"

"Yeah . . . ?"

"Well, I just wanted to ask how you're doing, are you going to be okay?"

"I'm alive. I'll live, you know, doin' as good as I can be. Who is this?"

"I'm just a guy that was out there at the scene that day, that's all."

Click.

Cards pour in from home over a thousand miles away. I see the face through the signature of each friend as I remember them from my past.

A friend of the family sent this one. I remember the smell of Frankie's house—dinner boiling and the bittersweet taste of sugar-mashed carrots-and-turnips. She was a kind woman. Her husband loved golf, and he couldn't walk from one end of the room to another without stopping to line up an imaginary shot. I picture him swinging through one.

I momentarily escape into the woods behind their house and away from this gagging oxygen that forces itself dryly into my nasal cavity. I play with their children again, and I sit on the weathered plank-dock of a neighborhood swimming hole, slowly lifting my feet through the murky water, staring into the vortex of tiny whirlpools that swirl through their wake. I remember the face of a friend, a neighbor boy who came to play. We both had Super Joe Commanders with the one-two punch. His voice goes off in my head, the last thing he ever said to me. "Maybe next time you come over I'll have a vehicle." I never saw him again.

Each card brings me to a different place in time; different places that even if only for a moment, release me from the grip of reality . . . I can see this one bouncing from office to office all around the Ocean Manor. "Did you sign the card for Chris yet?" Their voices call me from the names and wit folded inside. I punch out a sign that came with a funny card. *Of course I was in an accident, would I do this to myself on purpose?* I hang it proudly on the rigging.

Dear Chris

> *Just a letter to let you know that I hope you are getting better.*
>
> *I haven't told Amanda what happened to you. I figured when you feel up to it you could call her and tell her yourself. That way she will know you are OK.*
>
> *I figured if I told her that she would get really upset because she used to believe that you wouldn't come back and I didn't want to worry her.*
>
> *She misses you a whole bunch. She can't wait to go fishing and camping with you. I hope by then you will feel well enough to take her.*
>
> *She thinks you're the best. No one is nicer than her daddy because you let her get away with everything and do whatever she wants. She loves that about you.*
>
> *I think she wants to hear your voice soon. She's starting to realize that it's been a while since she's heard from you.*
>
> *I'm probably getting her pictures done I'll get some to you as soon as I can. Karen said RF is coming home some time next month probably.*
>
> *Jim and Mary still haven't had the baby.*
>
> *Amanda is learning how to spell some words. Some of the words in the letter she wrote she sounded out and spelled herself.*
>
> *I made you up a little Easter Basket and I don't know if you're even eating but I wanted to do it. I hope I remembered some of the things you*

liked if not sorry but it's been a long time. Amanda doesn't know about it because the Easter bunny hasn't brought her stuff yet.

Well I hope you are staying at least somewhat comfortable. I know it must be hard. But hang in there get better. Amanda will be waiting for you. And we both know how stubborn you can be when you want something (like getting better) bad enough.

Take care,
Love Laura.

I have a plain white folded piece of paper with an orange triangle glued to it.

to daddy

A Crayola-drawn border of oranges, bananas, cherries, and grapes follows inside a scalloped edge made with a paper-punch, a bed of flowers in the lower right corner, and in the lower left corner is what I like to call a park bench. Its colors match the rest of the artwork. I get a rush of pride in her artistic ability.

I LOVE YOU DADDY
I KNOW YOU LOOK
BAD BUT I STILL LOVE YOU

My gut twists until I think I'm watching myself turn inside out. My eyes and throat build an insurmountable pressure until my eyes begin to tear. Except for in my neck and behind my eyes I can't feel the pain in my body. I'm silent while screaming inside. Anger takes over for everything that's been stolen from me, and it keeps me sane.

I want to pick her up and hold her to me. I want to run beside her and play. I want to feel her fingers tighten on my waist as we turn down School Street on the Harley and feel them let go when she jumps out of the saddle, running to the swings at the Whitman playground where I ran as a child.

She was only two when I sat her in the saddle for the first time, her head looking ridiculously small inside the helmet. I strapped her to the sissy bar with my belt and her tiny fingers dug into my side as I started the bike. I carefully started up the street, and she shrieked with delight, "FASTER!" I twisted the throttle and popped the front wheel up. I felt her tiny hand slap my back. "NOT THAT FAST!"

It's over. These things I will only ever do again in memories. My knuckles turn white; my left hand locks a death grip on the bed's rail. A young physical therapy intern swings his happy clipboard through the door. "How about having a try at that arm today,"

"Not today. It's a bad day for me," I answer through clenched teeth, and a tear-snotted face. The back of my head begins to feel wet against the pillow.

Somehow I feel safer among strangers, free to let my own instincts drive the healing process, free from the anxiety of well-meaning relatives who would otherwise be there to bother the nurses for everything I don't want, or need, and torment my existence with advice on what I need to be doing for myself so they can feel better about themselves. If I want to lay here and wallow in my own grief, I can. I don't want to cooperate with my physical therapist. I'm having a bad day, and I can do that too. I can rely on me. No one else is going to heal me, or take the pain away. Most of them don't give a damn about me or my broken body. Sometimes I feel like just a paycheck, a teacher's aid, somebody's contorted idea of a miracle, but it's better to be in the company of strangers when someone else is wiping your ass—takes the edge off all the humiliation.

I have a friend who answers the call button most days. We have yet to actually meet, but her voice is flirty and risqué, almost a tease if not for the tin quality of the speaker. Sometimes I push the button just to hear Janet's voice.

I have a friend who comes in once in a while and lotions down my feet; they are thick with scale, blackening, and look like they might fall off. Katie's about my age and has a cheery southern accent. We share stories about what we've done, where we've been. Odd, I feel no shame in her presence, (although I feel bad that she has to touch my feet.) Somehow it's her station, and she is genuinely concerned. As I make friends here everyone becomes less strange to me, as though we were not just playing our parts and doing our jobs, as though there are a few I might never forget. Nurses are my kind of people. I worked side by side with them, knew them, understood what they went through on a daily basis, and had much respect for them.

I gurney my way to the whirlpool room, as I do every day. The usual girl attending me at the tub, (a physical therapist whose name I can't remember because they let me have an extra push of the magic button when I'm soaking) isn't here today; one of the many floating faces that come and go. The names can be elusive, but the faces never let me down.

Debris has to be soaked out my wounds little by little each day. It's also the only way to change the dressings that cling to the exposed tissue. Doctor Slade says if all goes well we may begin grafting in a couple weeks. There's no guarantee that they can even do that successfully; I could still lose the leg.

A bitter old man who I've seen from time to time and understood to be the head of the physical therapy department here at Halifax is attending me. His bedside manner sucks. The welcome sound of burbling water fills the stainless tank as he—he begins cutting at the outer layer of blood stained wrappings. "We're going to have to soak those bangages off the wound," I warned.

"These bandages don't need to be soaked, *I* can unwrap them just fine."

I was helpless to argue as he peeled at a corner of the bandage, but I figured being as old as he is, maybe he knew something more about bandages.

I wonder what he's going to do. He yanks like it is a Band-Aid on a child's knee. The morphine completely fails me. I scream bloody-blue-murder from the worst pain I ever felt in my life. People from all over run in to see the commotion; I can't speak a word through the white flashes, black splotches. Through waves of pain and fury inside in my head, he explains to the others, "I didn't realize . . ."

"What the hell is wrong with you?" someone asked.

My eyesight finally comes back "Now can we try soaking them, I told you . . ." He left the room. A nurse came in and gave me a shot of something to help the morphine along, and very gently hooked me up to the winch. I lowered into the stovepipe-echoing of bubbles in the tub . . .

The speaker clicks behind my head "Hey sweet cheeks, you decent?"

"Yeah Janet, but I ain't dressed."

"They'll be there in five for the tub room."

"Thanks doll, I'll be ready."

I'm on an air mattress that had to be shipped in special for the type of wounds I have. It has to be deflated so they can roll me onto a backboard and then slide me over to the gurney.

"Janet?"

"I'm still here."

"What day is this?"

Shawn was a travelin' man in every sense of the word, a hippie kinda guy with "Nelson" blonde hair. From as much as I gathered he made a living trading beads, hemp jewelry, and giving hair wraps to tourists on the beach. I met Shawn on the boardwalk during Bike Week 94. He was hanging out with a guitar man from an Orlando based band called Hemp. I'd stopped to listen. Shawn and I started talking. I mentioned to him in passing that I was staying at the International Inn, and they managed to find me. They offered a good bag of buds in turn for letting them crash, and that was the beginning of a friendship. We partied for a couple nights, dropped some acid, and they moved on.

Here he is again in the doorway of my room with a large pizza.

"Whoooa brooooo I am soooo sorry duuude. I went looking for you and the hotel chick told me what happened. I actually heard about it the day it happened, but I didn't know it was youuuu broooo, wwwwwoooowwww!"

His energy is tremendous, a happy thing, and it makes the world seem less menacing. He hands me a medicine bag, purple and yellow knit. There's a crystal, a bone carved skull, a moss stone, and an apache's tear.

He holds the crystal gazing into it dreamily, polishing it with his narrow thumbs. "Bro, this will help you. This holds a lot of good energy."

He hangs the bag from the traverse, and it dangles just within my reach. We finish the pizza, shoot the shit, and visiting hours were over several hours ago.

"Bro, I feel like shit having to ask you this but do you have any money for the pizza? I spent my last few bucks on it, and I don't even have smokes."

Luckily it's the thought that counts. I hand him five bucks, I'm happy to pay for the pizza. After all, it's the thought that counts. We shake hands, and he gives me a small wooden pipe—carved along its stem with the tired face of a bearded old wizard. He left back to Cali via Colorado by way of something called the Rainbow Gathering.

Everything is new to me; a brand new experience holds my interest like the eyes of a child. I am brought into the world for the first time again. As the days meld on, the novelty of my misfortune is old news to the world outside. I imagine the cars passing the hospital, stopping for the light then rolling past the strip malls until the next signal stops them again, the same road that took me to school each morning. I wonder how many guys from school even look up at the hospital any more, and think *Chris is still up there.* I fall asleep dreaming about the sound of cars hissing by my window—the flow of blood inside my ears that runs through my body to become the incessant pounding of my limbs.

I throw kindling for Master Gervais. A wood shop in town let him have their scrap for his fireplace—a full open hearth in the kitchen of a house built in the seventeen hundreds. First, I empty the barrels into either of two large bins, one of which was an old horse stall. The wood is in large, heavy cardboard drums that I half empty by hand before my 12-year-old arms can hoist them high enough to clear the bin-wall. I rake down everything in the back with a heavy iron rake so it's piled high against the front; he has trouble reaching into the bin when it gets low. The wood never stops coming. It's tedious work for the two dollars he will pay me.

I finish the chore and sit with him and his wife Priscilla at their kitchen table. They tell me stories drawn from their eighty plus years of loving life, taking turns correcting each other's memory and finishing sentences as the stories drag on. Some of them I've heard three times in the last few months, but I sit politely and listen. He saw action in WWI, she was his second wife, he recounts for me the first time he ever saw a motorcycle, it was the first time for everyone that day, and she remembers the date as being when he was in the Navy. Gervais remembers the advent of the wooden torpedo in warfare and what an awesome spectacle it was. He tells of fights with sailors in far off countries while I sat quietly drinking my milk and listening intently. "Now Priscilla, would you let *me* tell the story to the boy."

Time for me to leave. Priscilla, frail and hunch-backed, inches her way into the bedroom to get my two dollars from an ornate wooden box they keep on the dresser. Gervais pokes at the fire and throws a couple triangular pieces on the rejuvenated coals.

The fire roars, an alarm sounds. Their faces are no longer before me in the kitchen, but still there in front of me when my eyes open. Two nurses are working. One of them changes my IV bags, while the other is fidgeting with the pump. I smack my tongue against the roof of my mouth, cottony, my lips pursing to gauge their stickiness. I remember where I am.

Recognizing at which stage of the task they were, I said "You have to manually reset the rate every time." The girl looked at me sideways. The one hanging the bag watched our exchange injecting, "You should probably listen to him. He's been married to that pump for a month.

The girl looks at me with pity, and I try to ignore it. I try not to let myself feel as far gone as the look she continues to hold for the next two minutes. It reminds me of being at Nicko's restaurant two weeks after Nick passed. His wife was sitting at her new place—the end bar stool, Nick's chair. Loudly and foolishly a customer expressed sympathy for his passing. I watched her heart fall to the floor yet again as the well-meaning customer dramatically re-animated the sorrow that had barely begun to wane.

People suck. I ask the girl for some apple juice.

Soaking in the environment, I become the smell that lives and breathes. The same germicidal essence that settles itself in the hands of the people who mop my floor every day. Coming and going with their heads down, eyes on the floor, moving quickly. Sometimes they respond when I say hello, sometimes they just glance with a quick nod. Some days I long to speak. I watch them mop, swabbing under the bed rapidly, bending and stretching from across the room; like I'm a leper and this is the Middle Ages. I loathe the sight of them—rude that they are. Just tell me something, speak, acknowledge me as alive. Tell me something new, something trivial, something for my mind to churn. Something other than the color of the walls or the Betadine soaking through my bandages.

I'm the only one here for the long haul. Everyone comes and goes, the moon cycles, the sun sets, but time is irrelevant, as I am irrelevant, held impasse by forces that keep the world spinning outside my window. My days are measured by activities and rotating shifts. I know when it's night because the faces change.

"Hey sexy!"

"Hey Janet, Monday already?"

"Nope it's Tuesday."

"Where were you yesterday?"

"Called in sick."

The system I have isn't always reliable. I know it's one o'clock because they're here for my gurney ride to the tub-room. A ceiling's view tour of the building.

It's awkward looking up the noses of the people transporting me. There are only two things you can look at laying prostrate on a gurney, and sometimes I just get tired of counting light banks. Every one is tall and rushing around. The world outside the room is slanted and sideways. Sometimes they leave me in the hall in front of the nurse's station so I can howdyado everybody.

Today like every other, I released the air from my mattress—still a childish thrill. It's the only ambulant motion I execute on my own. The girls roll me on to the backboard, sliding me sideways.

AAAAArrrrrgggggghhhhh!

My voice takes off in the corridor, bouncing between the walls trying to escape a sudden attack of white-hot-agony. It churns my bowels, cramps race up my leg, and my eyes roll back into their sockets. The nurse in charge is mortified.

"Oh my god I am so sorry. What happened, are you alright? What can I do?"

"It's not your fault, my foot brushed against the knob."

"I'm so sorry I should have been paying attention."

"Really, it's not your fault. I don't understand how something so dead can hurt so much."

I feel guilty. It's harder to feel her remorse than my pain. My foot is hyper-sensitive, it just happened, no warning. The incessant pounding inside clings to the crawling seconds of every day. It never lets me forget—like John Henry looks for his eternal path through stone by hammering spikes through the top of my foot, but it was only my big toe that grazed the hard plastic knob.

"I wish they'd just cut it off."

"No you don't. One day you'll be glad you have all your parts, even if they don't work so well."

Ghosts move about through a fog-laced room—their bodies fracture as they travel. Their heads bubble up from the mist, each in turn—turning heads with stern dead faces to look on my naked soul like angry apparitions or faceless bearded trolls. They disappear through cracks in the floor and they whisper—chanting. I am the breath of the great gray mountain, come to rise on hot-wet air to kiss the tender bellies of moon-blown leaves laughing in the ears of lost mad children, holding hands as they fall through starless satin skies.

The voices subside and I am infantile in my dependency, in a flower speckled gown, my only dignity in a pale damp tub room. The chinclickita hoist, a cold, mechanical, winch driven chain, holds me briefly, above a churning germicidal bath, then submerges me in its healing to separate yesterday's dressings now fused to my raw inner tissues where skin once was, and muscle is no more. Across the room a man is learning to walk himself into his own tub of sorrow. In a nod of acknowledgment his eyes tell me, *I'm glad I'm not him.*

I can't imagine being him either. He's walking. Floating in turbulence I summon another twenty five CC's. Merciful vascular IV love.

Suddenly she appears, young and smiling, sitting at my side; her dress is the only color I've seen in weeks other than my own blood—a candy striper. She listens in awe, of my brush with death, and I to her. A girl's aspirations—my only link to the outside world. A faint point of hope. It is then I notice my gown drifting away beside me in the bubbles. Flushed and knee-jerk in embarrassment she leaves without a word, and the chinclickita hoist pulls my pruned carcass from the stainless tank, as my humility spirals down the drain below me.

It's April and I've had no visitors since James and his girlfriend Dianne were here . . . Was it two weeks ago? He's graduating in May, going back to Carolina. I don't like it. The hospital sends people to talk to me. I am removed, distant. The hospital's chaplain talks to me once or twice but, I give him little to run with. What do they expect from a person dedicating massive reserves of strength to ignoring pain? Do they think it's easy to lay here day after agonizing day reliving all the moments of my life just to remind myself that I probably deserved every bit of what came to me? Call it a vow of silence in the name of healing. I had little need for a man in a collar to be preaching the goodness of life.

My only source of pleasure comes from watching Chaz Parminteri's *A Bronx Tale*. TBS has been running it regularly for a couple weeks, and I glue myself to the screen. It brings me a great sense of self to watch the Bronx-Italian way of life. My own grandmother was a crazy Sicilian.

Calogero Anello explains to a girl he likes that Sicily is the island getting kicked by the boot. The grandmother I never knew was Sicilian and half mad from something like bi-polar disorder. I think her official cause of death was listed as Catholic guilt. She had a blind son, and no matter how many apparitions of the blessed virgin she chased, he remained blind. She saw it as her own failing.

I'm not religious despite the fact that I sang soprano in my Episcopal church's youth choir, and I was an acolyte. I sat in the bishop's chair looking forward as I always did, and a member of the choir, Mr. Allen, waved for me to stand by him, and I did, and he pointed in the hymnal so I would follow along and sing. I didn't. I just watched his finger traverse the page.

When I was serving and sitting in that chair behind the altar, it was a reason to not participate in prayer, or hymns, or any of the other sheep-leading activities that went on in church. I could sit up there and look down on everyone as they kneeled for communion. I took my own first communion without having taken their catechism classes. It was all such a crock of shit then, and now lying here, having been granted the gift of reincarnation, I still see no need for religion. I am who I am despite all the Jesus that pushes at me from all directions. Holy rollers come to my room to touch the "miracle man." There are always pamphlets and books being pushed at me about how everything will turn up roses if I can just find Jesus. Do people really think that following Jesus makes god proud? Jesus, I think, is something to be, not someone to follow. If he and I can both boast the gift of reincarnation, what does he have that I do not?

My doctors can't explain several things about my accident: the vital signs that were seemingly normal as they dragged my body from under the truck, the rate my bones heal, tissue regrowing at astonishing rates, it amazes them. They call my survival a miracle, and my body continues to heal at a miraculous pace. Some called it god. I think it's really about having something better to do with my time than to spend the rest of my life playing victim.

Just when everything falls into a comfortable routine, progress steps in. Dr. Slade makes preparations to begin closing the wounds. There's a baseball sized hole in the side of my knee, and almost half my left leg is missing its skin. Split thickness skin grafts are harvested from both anterior thighs. A blade slices razor thin strips of flesh and it's perforated into mesh and fixed to the damaged tissue with grafting staples. Like growing seeds on a windowsill, if the bandages dry up the graft won't take and we'll have to try again. There's no guarantee the process will work in the first place, but I have a 50/50 shot. I dread the thought of going under the knife for another series of operations, but at the same time this is good news. Anticipation and anxiety win out over the joy I should be feeling, so I concentrate on getting my taxes done.

In my stream of cards and well wishes also comes the reminder of burdens I left in Massachusetts—unpaid bills and back taxes for Uncle Sam. I spend the better part of two days trying to figure out the forms and how to fill them out right on the first try because I only have one form. I teach myself to write left handed, which I've been doing here and there signing various things for the hospital and my lawyer. Numbers are much easier. To my surprise after subtracting the back taxes owed, I'm rich! Not really, but four hundred dollars is coming my way, and added to the four hundred Brenda's bike run raised, I have more money than a guy going nowhere will need. I sign the form and hit the call button. I'd been looking for an excuse to press it.

"Nowwwww whaddyah want!" Janet snorts.

"Shut up and find me a couple of stamps you bitch!"

"Anything for you baby!" We laugh.

My back's against a tree, my feet rest on an old rotting log, when suddenly my foot jumps out and kicks it. A spasm, I think. A gray mole sits frozen, I assume stunned from the sudden flood of light, and his beady mole eyes and his mole little snout look almost as funny as his squatty odd legs, legs—like a little platypus.

Slowly so not to spook it I feel around at my side and find a stick. Looking into its little black eyes—they look like they're praying that I won't see it if it just kept still—I could see my reflection move across the tiny black pupils as I leaned toward it. I dart the stick out from beside me and bring it down on the rodent. A faint fleshy pop sounds, and its front legs flail.

Life fades from its eyes, dimming. I pull the stick out of the ground and study its blood-covered tip, and then I use it to press the mole's insides out of the hole. Starting at the head, I slowly roll the stick, disemboweling it.

My mouth is dry and my back is tight and cramped. My mouth is so dry I can hardly breathe. Everything is hazy, everything is wavy. I hear a distant voice calling me through a deep hollow canyon. I try to get up and run away. I don't want to get caught killing a mole . . .

"Mister Christie, you have to breathe deep for me now, big deep breaths."

I inhale, it is uncomfortable. It hurts, and my head begins to pound. The voice is close now, no longer in the distance. It's attached to a face that looks like it's on the other side of a wet windshield.

"Breathe deeply now," she says.

"Where am I?"

"You are in the recovery room at the Halifax Hospital Mr. Christie. You've just had surgery and all went well. Breathe again for me."

I choke on my breath, "thirsty." She shoves a lemon flavored swab stick in my mouth.

"I can give you some ice as soon as you get your oxygen level back up there."

I look down at my arm. It's tethered to a motorcycle engine lying on the floor. I can't move. Everywhere I look someone is going about their business completely indifferent to my objections or cries for help. They move about slowly as though wading through something thick, like pudding, or like stuck in slow motion.

I bite chunks of skin from my lip and spit them out through my folded tongue. My legs burn like fire ants have taken up residence inside the bandages. A nurse comes in and mixes a pitcher of Betadine solution. The mixture soaks through to my legs, quieting the insects.

It's up to chance whether or not the skin grows over my wounds. My legs are stained a dingy shade of burnt umber and itch something fierce. The wet wrappings make me cold, and the surgery sucks what little strength I had. It's a long cold ordeal recovering from what should have been progress in the right direction. Although it's a move closer to going home, I fall further into sadness, hopelessness, and depression. I'm a plant, doomed to occupy the same place in space until someone comes along and moves me; even with the change of view I find always myself in the same pot of dirt.

I finish breakfast and the charge nurse "charges" into the room with three other aids by her side. She looks determined.

"You need to start getting some blood moving in your legs. We're going to stand you up and put some weight on those feet."

It sounds like a logical thing to be doing. They swing my legs over the edge of the bed, and I feel light headed as gravity yanks on them, throbbing and burning. They ease my feet onto the floor. Pain. They support my back and try to shift my weight foreword. Pain. Blood seeps through the bandages. I scream. My body folds out from beneath me. The girls make sure I land on the bed, and they situate me as comfortably as they can.

The blood seeping through the bandages is to be expected. Having been on my back for so long, the sudden pressure in my legs forces the blood to surface and weep out the pores where they took the graft from my thighs.

I'm grateful to her though. The searing pain is easier to live with than the burden I'd been to her, and I'm thankful to know where I stand (or where I can't stand) with respect to my legs. Pain tells me that there's life, and pain is the only reminder I have that I am in fact alive. I grow tolerant to the everyday pounding and discomforts inside my body. I come to accept it as something I'll always have. The doctors are pretty sure of it, as sure as they are when they place my chances of spending the rest of my life in a wheelchair at highly probable.

It seems like a big game. Doctors tell the cripple he's doomed because they know it can only go one of two ways. Either I wallow in despair and accept my fate as such, or I fight simply because something inside me is not content to have my future dictated to me in such a way. Regardless of my outward impression—depression, withdrawal, silence—inside, I am always fighting, like there's someone else at the controls. Tripping out to anesthesia, going black, passing out. It never frightens me. I'm comfortable with not waking up; I know I will though, because of Him.

A team of doctors and nurses come with a large hydraulic table. It will acclimate me to a standing position. Strapped in each day, it raises me higher and higher until I can stand on my own two feet. The blood, however, doesn't stop seeping through the bandages.

There's nothing more that can be done for me at Halifax. I'm daunted by decisions of what I'm going to do next. They're sending me back out into the world. I will be returning to Massachusetts and to my parents' house.

My other option is to check into a rehab hospital in Florida, but it isn't in my cards. My insurance won't cover it, and it's unknown what kind of money, if any, was going to be paid by the trucking company's insurance. Rick mentioned the truck was insured for a million dollars only the day before the accident. No one can say how much time I need to rehabilitate. I can't bear to be confined to another hospital. Dr. Acker estimated an eight-year recovery.

It's great to be well enough to leave, but even though it's good to be getting out of the hospital I'm not looking forward to facing what's ahead. I make trips to the physical therapy room to get ready for discharge. I'm all fucked up. I needed a walker, but only have one arm to use it, so I use a Hemi Walker. My foot has no dorsi-flexion. It just points down, and I trip over it constantly. It's a left leg/right arm disability, and it robs me of balance. I stagger around the room, and I even make it up a few steps.

Up is the only place left to go from here. Any further down and I'll be in the ground, which is an option that lingers in the back of my mind late at night when the halls are silent of all but the growling of IV pumps and television.

I think about death in the afternoon sometimes, when the waft of lunch rises from the inside of the chrome plate cover. The nurse tries to sound optimistic about how good it looks. I think about death as a way to pass the time while waiting for the waves of pain to subside, but they never seem to. They only lessen in intensity or yield to a successful morphine rush. I think about death because I'm supposed to be dead. People aren't supposed to come back from the other side, but I had and the why of it plagues me.

The discharge train starts rolling, and nothing I do will stop it. The security of the hospital is being taken from me as uncontrollably and abruptly as I found my way inside. Nothing is in my own hands. Every day for about two weeks there have been interviews, instructions, papers to sign, and things to prepare for. Everything has been handled for me;

thinking about it generates the same anxiety as though I were left to worry about it all by myself.

There is wound care, and arrangements to be made in the way of visiting nurses, hospital equipment rentals, physical and occupational therapy. I fill out forms to begin the process of obtaining SSDI, my transportation, arrange the use of wheelchairs, the airline.

With about half of the money that was raised for me by Brenda through my benefit poker run, the hospital purchased me a one-way ticket home. Home—the word has little meaning for me. I am returning to a home that I came to Florida to get far, far away from. I am being sent back, ruined, defeated, and helpless. I am leaving a place that I had come to think of as home. My address—room 910, where I am somebody.

May Eighth. I have lived to see my 25th birthday.

The staff packs things into a suitcase for me: restraints, splints, masks, tubes, staple pullers, bandage scissors, and bandages of all kinds. I'll need bandages for months to come. We all have a piece of cake and laugh about things we remember about our time together. All the equipment that was used in the course of my stay has to leave with me because of the infection risk precaution. I can't recall when some of the devices were used or what others even are. It all goes north.

I place a left handed signature on one form after another— acknowledgements that things were received and acknowledgements that the acknowledgements were signed for. I'm debriefed for the last time about the discharge plan. It seems like it doesn't matter whether I know what's going on or not. It's going to happen whether I want it to or not. I date the papers May 13th.

A transporter walks me outside and my eyes sting a little. I wince into the bright sunlight. The air smells like an old familiar friend, but everything else smells new and unfamiliar. I take a minute to place the smell of hot tar. I fill my lungs—automobile exhaust.

The world looks daunting at half my height—I smell fast food cooking. Getting into a wheelchair isn't an easy thing. I move along by using my right leg to kick and left arm to roll. I look like a crippled Igor, the Hunchback of the Chair. I'd been going through the motions almost daily in preparation for this very day. I transfer wheelchairs. I struggle. My glutes are sore from the pressure. I suck up the pain and settle into the other chair. It's narrow and uncomfortable. The driver pauses to look at the blood spotting through my bandaged legs before operating the lift and locking the chair into the van.

My legs throb, and my feet bang like they're being hit with ball-peen-hammers. My entire backside feels like it got hit by a truck. My gluteals ache from the pressure, and the back of my leg throbs, burns, and stings. Fresh graft covers my missing bicep but has hardly taken hold. It feels like I am being slowly skinned alive. My right arm is still atrophic. A ball of gauze tape I crammed into my fist falls out of my right hand, I forgot it was there. I had worked my way up from the toothpaste tube to a tennis ball size object. I can squeeze it with my fingers—barely.

I take two Vicodins as the driver pulls out of the parking lot. Daytona International is only a five minute drive, and I'm already exhausted. I wish the pills would kick in.

A girl smokes a cigarette in front of the airport. It doesn't even smell good, but I think about starting again. With hardly the strength to roll a chair, I discount the notion. I look forward to being home for one reason. Yesterday I called my brother to make sure there will be a fat bag of weed when I get there.

I transfer to the airport's wheelchair in the loading zone. It's awkward, stiff, and uncomfortable. I'm a spectacle as someone wheels me through the airport, and it's embarrassing as everyone looks down at me. Everyone looks. People stare at me. Pity. They turn away when I look back. I feel conspicuous. The pills start numbing me, so I take another one for good measure. It seems like I have been sleeping for hours when two big guys wake me up and transfer me to a skinny seat with wheels. I jostle over the threshold into the 737.

I woke up, and I was the only one on the plane. Seconds later my girlfriend, Amy walked through the bulkhead with two big dudes and the skinny chair. Outside a hired car and driver waited to take me to my parent's house. Lying across the back seat was the only way I fit into the Lincoln. This was what I had to look forward to in life: to be cumbersome, uncomfortable, exasperated, needful. I popped my fifth pill in as many hours. My neck cramped.

I didn't have the strength to deal with it all, but I smiled, and my sense of humor was in full gear. Wit was the only skill I had that made me feel somewhat human. I was so glad to be home, yet it was the last place I wanted to be. Acclimation began as soon as I got there. I met my wheelchair—black and clumsy. I didn't want to sit—the pain, helplessness.

Get away from me, all of you. "I can do it myself." The seat pressed against the back of my thigh as I eased down into the creaking new chair. My father and cousin David carried me like furniture into the house. I was a 160 lb. lump of uselessness. A nurse from the VNA arrived to go over my care plan: PT, OT, wound care, hygiene, bedside commode. FUCK ME! My head spun, and all I could think about was getting the weight off my hammering, burning, screaming leg. The pain took my entire body. My ass hurt, and the small of my back. I couldn't hold myself upright any longer; I took another pill, then bed. Amy locked the bedroom door behind us.

"One last thing before I go." She straddled my hips and we waited to see what would happen. I wanted to know for myself, had to know. Until that moment I feared the subject all together. I still didn't know if I was sexually capable. It never came up in the hospital, and I never thought to ask. The world melted away, and pinned helplessly to the bed, if only for a moment, I forgot all about the pain.

For the next nine months I spent my days alone, as everyone else had a station in life, places to go, and things to do. I was trapped in a cage and shackled. My first day alone in the house I dropped a block of cheese on the floor. It was agony to reach for it. I tried until I got dizzy. I stabbed it with a butcher knife instead—improvisation became a daily chore. My trips from the bedroom were few at first, and each trip presented new obstacles, but I learned by doing, and doing, and re-doing if that's what it took. The hardest thing to accomplish was relearning how to wipe my ass left handed while trying to convince my body it could bend in such a way.

My brother hooked me up with a fat bag of weed, and every night at midnight, five nights a week; we'd light up and watch the Time Life infomercial for their classic rock mega-album series. I smoked daily, but it did little to ease the pain. It did more to keep my mind occupied through day after day of boredom and loneliness.

Cousin Dave drove me to my first appointment with my new orthopedic doctor. It was agony sitting there uncomfortable and in pain waiting to be seen. The waiting room was over-crowded, and I felt guilt for tying up David's afternoon with something as simple as getting myself to the doctor. The longer we waited the worse I felt. I grew dizzy with passing waves of nausea. An hour after my scheduled appointment, I was finally seen. My new doctor bent and prodded as I explained Dr. Ackers repair job. All the while I wondered, what could he do? I was healing as fast as time would allow. I was relegated to the waiting game. He did tell me he wasn't going to give pills to anyone who had been out of the hospital for two weeks. Was he fucking nuts? I was still bleeding and obviously in pain, and that was his plan? No pills? What a fuckin' sadist. I never went back to that doctor, or any doctor. I resorted to the only means of pain control at my disposal—Vodka—but even that did nothing to quell the constant hammering inside my foot.

"One. Two. Three." I leaned out of the chair. The family watched as I tumbled into Dave's swimming pool not sure if I'd sink or swim. Falling through the surface I braced for what I thought was going to be a great wave of pain. None came as I submerged in the pool, and it felt incredible—even with the floaters inflated around my arms. I gimped through it, and could hold my head above water as muscles I forgot I had started working again. Getting out of the pool was a bit more of a chore. We rigged up a cinder block and a plank to use as a lever to lift me from the water onto the deck. I crawled back into the chair. There was some pain, not the pain of nerve fire, but of working muscles and fatigue. Later that day my left foot twitched in a spasm of nerve-fire, and I could move it again. Although it was weak and had no dorsi-flexion, it was a good sign.

Through the VNA I was admitted to a rehab hospital. I spent two weeks in hell at New England Sinai trying to get "rehabilitated." I should have known it wasn't a good idea. On the way there my grandmother's car was flanked by eighteen-wheelers. I broke down. Not knowing whether to shit or go blind, I just hyperventilated.

Leaving the house was depressing. It was hard for me to hear the sound of a Harley and worse to find myself riding in the car behind one. I shed tears for the loss of freedom. At AMI I took all the unnecessary accessories off my bike. I stripped it down. No gauges, no turn signals—I tore off everything that had nothing to do with making it go. My wheelchair got the same treatment. I removed the arm rests and the leg prop, and it looked rugged, but all the customization in the world wasn't going to make up for the fact that I still couldn't get myself from point A to point B.

Motorcycles were part of Amanda's life too. I agonized over trying to imagine how she was affected by what happened. She looked at me with her baby blues and asked, "What happened to all the good times?" Her eyes showed longing.

"What good times are you talking about?" I couldn't imagine. Her brokenhearted voice cracked.

"You know, the motorcycles and going riding in the woods."

It was hard to recover from that. I hadn't realized there were times in our life she thought of as good times. I largely saw myself as having let her down. Not being there for her, running off to Florida, it was the bane of my conscience. Now I was contending with being a source of sorrow. Depression was a large part of healing.

Being in the hospital again put me into a serious depression. I couldn't smoke weed, and I had no vodka. They spent more time trying to figure out how to treat my unusual disabilities—running tests, trying new things—than they did actually treating them. I spent my nights rolling the chair up and down the hallway. It was all I could do to keep myself from screaming. I had stores of energy that kept me awake through the night. Anxiety had me wired. The guy in the bed next to me played with his own shit.

After about a week of festering they asked me to take a bath—as if they thought not showering was my own choice. I was kinda ripe. My right arm was, for the most part, still atrophic, with its pit sealed off from fresh air. My wounds still bled and drained, and it dried on my skin. It was humiliating, but I'd grown accustomed to that. Nobody told me a bath was an option, and I didn't want to put anyone out by asking. I was elated when they brought it up. The hospital's tub room was being used for storage, and the tub looked like it hadn't been used for decades; it was dirtier than I was. The orderly cleaned it, and the all too familiar hoist lowered me in.

Only one person at New England Sinai was any help to me. A physical therapist took me to the staircase at the back of the ward and locked my chair at the top of it. I'd done three short steps back at Ma's house with the VNA girl, but this was fourteen black, steel, steep steps. I had made it up a small riser in the PT room back at Halifax, but this was for real. This would break me if I fell, and there was no one spotting on either side. I was secretly afraid of falling and not sure why. Was it the pain, or was it the embarrassment?

"Go down the stairs," she said as a matter of fact.

I hesitated, rose, and went half way down.

She called, "Now turn and come back."

I did. I got to the top with my last ounce of strength, and sat in the chair.

"He's independent! I don't know what the hell he's doing here, he's god damn independent!" She yelled at the people peering through the doorway. She was agitated. With me or with her co-workers, I couldn't tell, but I wanted out of there. She confirmed what I knew from the start. I didn't need to be there. During my stay I was given a battery of tests, prodded with needles, dipped in hot paraffin, bent, contorted, and experimented on. I was fitted for a foot brace that would hold my foot up, but the shoe looked like something someone's grandfather wore. I never wore it, but just learned to lift my leg a little higher when I walked.

I had no doctor, and I canceled my VNA appointments. The rehab hospital was a waste of time. I returned home much to the fright of everyone around me. I was going it alone. My family harped on me about giving up, not caring, failure, worry, drama, worry. Maybe they were tired of the stench that filled the house every night when my mother emptied the bedside commode for me—as if it wasn't bad enough with it next to my bed all day, stirring it up made the house smell like raw sewage. I relied on myself because I knew what I had to do for *myself*. My plan included two phases. Phase one, lose the wheelchair. Phase two, make sure I finish phase one. I didn't want to hear what I should be doing, how I should be doing it, or anything else about myself that people thought they knew better. Did I do my exercises? Did I remember to wear my brace? "You've got to come out of that room." There was no where to go. Was it too much to ask of people to knock before busting in? Trapped, I withdrew, turning inside myself for friendship. I was all I had.

It was made clear to me that I was "sponging" from my father and unwelcome in his house. I could hear him yelling about it but never to me. He and my mother were fighting over a divorce. He was cruel, manipulative, and criminal, but my mother was blind with grief. She wanted not to "create hard feelings," so she refused to take legal action as he bled their life's savings, sold their possessions, and planned to leave her holding the bag on a home and business that was mortgaged to the nines. I was in the middle of it, literally. My bedroom was in the middle of the house, so I heard it from both ends. He said, she said, and the late night phone calls between my father and his girlfriend.

Out of nowhere James called and said he was bringing my wrecked motorcycle to Massachusetts. I thought I'd never see him again. Along the way he found a buyer for my bike (luckily the motor was intact and it ran), so instead he had fifteen-hundred-dollars to give me. We spent several days sightseeing and wheeling my ass all over the place. His mission in life was me. It sucked when he had to go back to Carolina.

For fifteen-hundred-dollars I bought a computer: 486 DX 33, Duel 3.5" floppy drives, printer, and speakers. It was more power than anyone had ever imagined having at their fingertips. Friends and neighbors came to marvel at the machine. A parade of people came through my room. Everyone was so awestruck by the technology of the screen-saver boobies, I never had to go into detail about the computer itself. Learning DOS lent some reprieve to the monotony of being alive.

I was also being investigated. People I knew told me they were getting calls from investigators asking questions. One of them accidentally called me thinking I was someone else on his list until he realized who he was actually talking to, a big legal mistake on his part. Another time, my neighbor challenged two men in the woods behind his house, and they identified themselves with badges and said they were watching my house. I supposed that if I was applying for disability, they had a right to know who they were giving the money to. Maybe it was the insurance company looking for any angle to avoid coughing up a settlement. I was constantly under the microscope—it was an uneasy feeling.

Rick Tresher, my lawyer, was working hard and keeping me posted. Nine months passed before negotiations began in settlement of my case, and on the day of my hearing I was on the phone all day with the rapidly changing terms of the agreement. The speed at which Rick settled the case was a miracle in itself, and it came none too soon. I had applied for disability once, and after dragging my ass to the Social Security office, bloody bandages and all, they refused me a second time—I couldn't walk more than a few shaky steps, I couldn't stand up for more than a couple minutes, and my right arm was ornamental at best. I sat in the waiting room listening to someone who gave me a sob story about being too nervous to work. They'd refused me for SSDI because it's supposedly protocol to refuse everyone three times, which at that point warrants a hearing. I understood their caution, but what did it take to get benefits? Getting hit by a truck obviously wasn't working.

I applied for and was approved to receive EAEDC (emergency aid for the elderly, disabled, and children). It was aid money that had to be paid back. Applying for that was a hardship in itself, trying to navigate the wheelchair un-friendly city of Brockton, MA. There I was, crippled in the welfare office, and probably the only one in the place who was qualified for benefits, but because I needed help I wasn't getting any. I was in anguish over my financial situation, desperate even, but by the end of the day Rick had secured my future beyond anything I could have imagined. I proudly called EAEDC and cancelled their check. Now what?

My girlfriend and I parted company. The relationship was a casualty of the situation. There was no break up, no hard feelings, nothing. It was eerie but not uncommon. When two people are connected through a traumatic event, the relationship inevitably ends. Perhaps we were just instruments in each others lives.

"I'm just going to try to be a better person," was the answer I gave my mother when she asked me what I was going to do with all the loot. For a brief moment I considered buying her house, but that was my father's mess. No, as soon as I was able I bought a 27' mini-motor-home. I bought a Rottweiler named Dakota, and he loved escorting me wherever I went. We drove straight to Winston-Salem. I spent the next few months camped out at the top of James' driveway. I had to teach myself how to live again, and James helped with that. He got a few of his brothers together and they lifted me onto the back of his FLH. It was bittersweet as we rode through Winston-Salem to the bank. I transferred money to buy a Chevy SS pickup. It was coming together like when I was a child and boasted that all I would need to be happy was a pickup truck and a dog. When I mentioned this to my mom she reminded me that I always spoke of a black dog. Dakota fit that model. I realized I was on a path.

By the spring of '95 I was back in Daytona, Holly Hill actually, but what's the difference. I pulled my camper into a shady little crack-park on Ridgewood Ave. The owner of the park nearly fell over when I wrote him a check for a year's rent up front. It wasn't hard to fit in; I just kept a .38 in my belt and hobbled around like I owned the place. It wasn't hard to pick up where I left off either. Brenda from JJ's pub was a local, connected, and helped me establish myself. I was walking better and better with each passing day. I came to realize that getting on with life was the best way to approach rehabilitation. I figured out how to get things done for myself, or I went without.

Everywhere I went people knew who I was. People bought me drinks and told me stories of how they were in some way connected to someone who knew a guy who was the brother of an EMT who was there at the scene of the accident. Some even remembered what they were doing at the time. Minor celebrity status quickly engulfed me.

I spent my days sleeping, evenings waking up, and nights in the bars. I always had the best weed in Daytona, and smoked it freely. I'd go out for the evening with cigarette packs full of joints and not know where I'd end up throughout the course of the night. Everyone smoked with me. Everyone thought they knew me. People at the bars would see me slip out the back door and before I knew it there was a crowd. I ran with a crowd. The city was crowded, and it stank. I grew weary of weeding out the assholes. Line 'em up, take 'em down. Nobody seemed to measure up. I whittled my social life to a tight inner circle. I was still in the wheelchair most of the time, but with a cane could limp my sore ass in and out of where I needed to be—mostly on bar-stools. My life was not spiraling out of control despite its appearance. I was very much in control, directed, and focused. I accepted that what I was doing with my life at that point was about all I could be doing—the doctor gave me eight years, and I was doing exactly what I had to do—recovering, healing.

One asshole owed me money, and didn't have it, so I acquired a motorcycle. Before I knew it, I was in the wind again. I rode a 47 knuckle, suicide shift—rocker clutch, low & slo. It was a one-kicker and if it didn't catch the first time, it always would when the fly-wheel came back around. I could ride that sled better than most people walk, better than I could walk.

Sisko became one of the few people I could tolerate. He had a 48 pan; mine was the last year for the Knuckle, his the first year for the Pan. He worked as a bar-back at JJ's pub at the time of my accident. In a twist of small world fate we met again. He was a hillbilly from West-By-God-Virginia. I kept him out of jail; he watched my back.

My dog Dakota was kind of dating a girl named Beth, but I saw her first. I met her at one of Sisko's nightly back-yard-beer-fests; she'd just got into town by way of Indiana. She was a laugh-out-loud and tell-it-like-it-is girl. We clicked right away over a chuga-jug of homemade Kahlauah. Beth loved big dogs and started taking Dakota for walks on the beach and roller-balding. It was well needed exercise that I couldn't give him. Letting him pull my chair through the park was about as much as I could do for him.

Dakota liked Beth, and I guess that was good enough for me. She had a falling out with her roommates, and I figured it was alright if she stayed with us. Six months and a lot of denial on my part later, it turned into a relationship. I erred on the side of caution. Eventually we grew weary of living among dregs. All kinds of crazy shit happened all around us every day. Crazy crack heads sold themselves on the streets. A fifteen-year-old girl we knew was selling herself on the street. Kids were hanging themselves, people getting beat up—survival of the fittest played a part of every day life. We always had our guard up. Some asshole hit me on my knucklehead as I pulled into traffic in front of the trailer park, clipped my front end, down I went. I laid there and screamed. "Beth, Beth, Beth." She came.

"Who hit him?"

She was pissed. I smelled gas. Calmly I said, "Pick up the bike." The guy that hit me stepped over to do it, and Beth almost launched him as she pushed him out of her way.

"Don't touch that bike," she glared, and stood it upright like it was a toy.

Sisko mysteriously pulled up on his pan and watched from the sidewalk. I was on my way to his place. I did a thorough once over of my body to make sure nothing was broken. Bystanders started panicking about me not moving in case anything was broken, but Beth took my hand and pulled me to my feet. I dusted my jacket, picked the seat up off the ground, and bungee corded it back onto the bike. The policeman arrived on scene and spoke to the driver who hit me. I couldn't hear what he was saying, but I thought he was being told who he had just hit. The cop spoke to the man for a while. Then the cop shook my hand, and it was over. I rode off with bent handle-bars.

Later that day Sisko and I rode out past JJ's Pub out on 92. Someone had the morbid audacity to rename it *The Crash Site*. That was me, Crash. Ironically it was the name someone gave me back in Massachusetts. I *was* crash. Since I'd been involved with motorcycles, there had been five in as many years. The first, only weeks after I bought my sportster, found me sprawled over the hood of an elderly man's car, still holding the handlebar to keep the bike from toppling. Then there's the one in an intersection while taking a left. Someone didn't see me, and down I went to avoid impact. I felt the car's rear quarter panel brush against my hair as I fell. Next, "The Accident." Then someone T-boned my pick-up truck out in the Ocala National Forrest and sent it spinning. Finally, the hit I took on the knucklehead.

Beth mentioned maybe getting a place somewhere outside the city, someplace a little bigger than my RV. Her face dropped when I told her we could just move to my place in Ocala. "You have a house?!" she said, As if the boat I kept in the empty slip next to the camper was my entire life's savings. No, luckily I remembered not to piss *all* the cash away. The boat was actually my idea of physical therapy. It was a lot like a tilting platform stage they use in physical therapy called a Balance Master, only mine was more fun. I had bought a house on Lake Weir adjacent to my uncle's place, my "retirement home." We packed up and left Daytona behind us.

I came to be in this life in a cellar at the Sisters of Jesus Crucified and the Sorrowful Mother, a convent hidden in the Hills of western Massachusetts where Ones in black told me I was supposed to dwell in silence. As a condition of my parents' marriage, the Roman Catholic church demanded forfeiture of their first son to the priesthood—penance for the sacrilege of befouling my father's catholic place beside god. I was that son.

Her face is long, contorted, crying. Her eyes—swollen, dark, round. Behind her, a wall of stone seeps with fever. She moves sideways into a light that hurts my eyes. Her face darkens, now featureless, and I can look at the light with no reservation.

Her dark arms reach out. Two in black appear behind her, the light leaves, they usher her away. If only for a heartbeat I am cursed to know prefect love, suckling from young girls who come to the cellar to be washed of their shame. The ones disowned, forgotten; for penance, they nourish me. Milk grows bitter on my soft new tongue, but the turning of each season brings the taste of a fresh new girl.

Ones in black are never pleasant, but they treat me only with casual disregard; however, my nurses are beaten, and through the stones, muddled in the damp drafts that linger on the walls, I hear them crying. They are made to bed with the One in black they call Mother.

My nurses never hold me, but I feel desire reaching through their naked finger tips. I taste shame through their pallid nipples. Their thoughts torment me; a maternal need to love, the futility of allowing themselves to do so. They look into my face, and I smile, but I am rewarded in tears that stain my fatted cheek. I realize they all have the same eyes. I think of the contorted face, the face turned to shadow before the sweetest of bitter light. Two in black came to take her. It is her eyes I see inside them. They have not their own.

Sometimes the cry of a new child echoes from the gray stone walls, but shortly it is silenced. Mine is the cry that never fades. Where is it that the crying goes when their voices are gone? All that is left is my own. It echoes through lightless corridors. I lay awake nights, imagining they are with the shadow, the fallen face I remember.

Children leave in the dim glow, sometimes seeping through a hole in the wall when the Ones in black are scurrying about my room—a glint of reflection—the foot or forearm. A crying child clinging—the hulking shadow's form. These images flash before me just before I'm left alone in the great stone room—again.

Sometimes I hear only my heart beating. Then the sound of my own voice speaks to me from inside the wall, and I think the stones *are* voices. One of them is mine, I sound older. Am I trying to send myself messages from the future? I never understand what I mean. My own heart beating, I never understand. I am said to be heartless.

I move about the room, dark, it always is, but I learn to see with my knees. There is a place where the stones are not rough or cold, and I fall on it. I move through the wall, claw with my fingers, my nails are ground to bloody stumps. A distant glow grows brighter. I approach, I breech.

There were four of them sitting at a table. They were not in black but fragile, pale, and bare. My nurse is facing me, down on the table, head hung over the edge. She looks up. Her eyes scream for mercy, but her smile—sardonic. I am afraid—horror courses through my veins for the first time. Her arms are bound to the table, one is bleeding. Her leg is severed.

I hear two steps beside me. Rivers of urgency rush in my ears—I am flying through the air, I am back inside the stone room again. Two in black speak briefly. They wash the walls with darkness, and it seals the hole I escaped through. I am alone again.

I am brought to the surface—bathed, warm, and bright. I cover my eyes; the radiance burns the hair on the back of my hands. It smells putrid. Two in black are speaking to a third who is different than they, bitter, domineering. They are softer, subordinate. The Third in black grabs my arm.

"So this is *Him* is it?"

He throws me like an old naked rag doll into the hopper of a wooden ox-drawn cart. He flickers the switch over the backs of beasts. Ones in black grow smaller behind us; they dig into the dirt furiously with their fingers. They return below the surface through the hole. The ox-cart-driver turns to me with ocher, crooked teeth as the cart hops over a bump, and my body jolts from the rough wooden boards.

B eth was attending Central Florida Community College, and I had a small investment in a music store, Dirt Cheap Music in Belleview. We picked up a friend for Dakota too, and my daughter Amanda named her Dutchess. While Beth worked on a math degree, I studied guitar and sold instruments . . . Dirt Cheap. I wasn't in it for the money. It was the only place I felt comfortable, the one place I found acceptance, friends. It was my ghouls 1,2,3, when my life had become a game of hide and seek. Rick Baylog was the owner, Chas taught me guitar, and I just hung around. I was always comfortable with artistic types. We helped each other through life, Cheech-and-Chonging our way through the late '90s.

People were getting weird. My family looked at me with contempt and hatred. They made nasty comments like, "So what, now you're living off your father's money?" I was berated for not having a job: "What the hell's wrong with you?" "You can walk!" I didn't know what it was, perhaps jealousy. Did they think mine was easy money? Was my life enchanted? Beside the settlement with the trucking company, I was also granted 100 percent disability and fully qualified for SSDI. The hearing was in Daytona. I was financially independent. I realized I was different, and no matter what I did, I would always be different from everyone else in that respect.

In a world where people relate to others in terms of work and reward, I found myself without an identity. In social situations of mixed company I dreaded the inevitable question, "What do you do?" What could I say? I'm a professional accident victim? I suffer daily with aches, pains, and disability, and for this I'm paid a generous salary of fixed income? There was nothing I could say that placed me in a general air of familiarity to others. I was a survivor, the implications of which were intangible to nearly everyone I encountered. I was building my own success story from the ground-up, literally. Sometimes, for shits and grins I'd invent a career. Beth and I once convinced a party that I was a urinal-cake salesman.

Despite the tragedy my life became I had a great measure of inner peace. There was no debilitating crisis in my life that prompted drama, and maybe this was where people found me to be intimidating. For all I had stacked against me I was happier and more content with me than most people will ever know. For all I suffered and was suffering I still thought it was better to be me than anyone else I knew. I was alone on top of my own gray mountain and with each passing day was more content to be there.

I lived daily with more pain than most people could tolerate. They'd ask what it was like. I'd say, "If you were to suddenly feel what I am feeling right now, you'd be banging on the doctor's door." I thought people were too fragile for their own good. I scared them in that to look at me was to realize that given the same deck of cards, they doubted their ability to play.

My leg drained through a small hole in the grafted skin; it seeped unsightly ooze. I still relied heavily on the chair, and although I was able to sit for extended periods, there was always an uncomfortable pressure against my backside. The ooze would stick to my clothes and in turn the clothes to the chair. There was a sting as the material separated from my grafting. I needed a cane to walk, but I was supposed to be using it in my right hand. I couldn't do that with the nature of my injuries. Some days I couldn't walk at all. I woke up some mornings with no warning that I would be unable to move and in agonizing pain before I even swung my leg out of bed. My ragged sciatic nerve left me feeling like there was a bullet lodged in my pelvis. The amount of strength it took to use the cane in my left hand was crippling. My arm started waking me up at night, a numbing pain I thought was a heart attack the first time it hit me. I eventually stopped using a cane to walk and adopted my trademark limp in favor of being able to use my left arm. Eventually I lost the ability to do the one thing I'd grown to love; even though strumming my guitar helped improve the flexibility in my right wrist, it also caused great pain in the left arm. I was slowly regaining the use of my right arm, but the hand was taking longer. I could hook a couple grocery bags on it, and I could write with it. I drove myself crazy because there was little feeling in the hand, and I'd forget about small objects I was holding until they slipped from between my fingers, and picking things off the floor was nearly impossible.

I never showed disability to anyone on the outside, and I never complained. I kept going, often pushing my limits to the point agony. There was something inside me discontent to linger at the bottom of the food chain. He drove me to the edge of tolerance every time, and when the pain became intolerable, with nothing else to do but shut myself inside and cry, He would get pissed off, and I somehow kept going. It was like the old adage . . . Doc, it hurts when I move my arm . . . Then don't move your arm. But that was bullshit. I needed to know the pain.

Even after moving away from Daytona I had to relive the story everywhere I went. People introduced me to their friends, tourists, vacationers. They spit out the intro and out of politeness I'd continue with details. I felt like a freak-show announcer. Hurry! Hurry! Step right up. See the amazing miracle man of Daytona Beach who came back from the grave to tell the tale to all the looks of horror, pity, and disbelief the masses can muster. Seemingly everyone was familiar with the accident to some degree. They saw it on the news, or they heard it from a friend. It seemed like I couldn't move far enough away from Daytona to escape it all. Most bike shops in the nation employed AMI graduates, and to quote one I once met who was way too happy to meet me, "Dude, you are a legend." But all I needed to do was look down at my arm and the zipper was right there. Every time I looked in a mirror, put on my shoes, shook someone's hand, I was reminded by the scars of everything I'd endured. The words "The Accident" popped into my head every day of my life. It became as much a part of me as the shape of my face. I'd have traded it all back to be whole again.

I was trying to build a 57 pan frame up, but I was growing tired of the Harley scene. To me it wasn't worth wading through the ocean of assholes, con-men, and stupid whores (hanging around the assholes and con-men) that came with the territory. The first day of school at AMI they warned us, "Believe nothing of what you hear and only half of what you see." They were right. I couldn't do it any more. My health was deteriorating. Every day of my life I was somehow reminded of the accident. I couldn't escape it.

In the middle of it all a well-meaning uncle talked me into becoming involved with Amway, and I swore that I would use it to buy the Presidency of the United States. I figured that *must* be what it was all about. The Corporation, the machine, god, love . . . It's all about money, and for most of the people in the world around me money was the measure of self. It made me ill. I had no need of what Amway was offering, but I thought I was getting in it to help him out. I should have seen it coming.

I saw myself as a mad scientist setting my whole life up as some big experiment to see if Amway really worked. I called everyone on the pyramid but never reached the great and knowing eye. Everyone denied it was there. Beth started calling me an "Amway Nazi," and she tried not to follow me into madness. She was beside herself trying to keep me here on earth while at the same time trying to get through college.

The world had become transparent, and it was my calling to paint it black. I became obsessed and out of control with philosophy and thoughts on god. I start keeping a notebook.

I am the second coming, and god is inside my temples pounding mercilessly with the blinding light.

"E=MC^2. Can you help me?"

"I sure can," replies a woman on the other end of the telephone at the psychic friends network. If anyone can help me, *they* can.

"Then you will howl like a mad man at the moon with me!" Ha ha ha ha ha ha.

"I sure will, and Sir, I see good things happening for you in April."

April, if I could have just held on 'til April. I had the entire meaning of the universe in front of me, and Einstein's theory was in my head so clearly. It was obvious to me how it all fell into place and from it I derived other insane theories and wrote them all in the notebook: the theory of infinite smallness, a theory of Tri-Sapiens as being the next evolutionary level of intelligence of man, thoughts on god and the order of the universe, all so clear. Everything in existence came down to two possible connections, the positive and the negative. In my own edict of declaration I proclaimed, "There will be no negativity in my life!"

I stood over Beth who is cowering on the bed as I scream at the top of my lungs. "You are saved and you don't even see it. Beth, help me, I am crying for you, you are chosen! Don't you understand, the dogs, the dogs are the key to it all!"

I sat in a room on whose door I have plastered a sign, "War Room," and I wrote wildly in my notebook. It was the master plan. It was the manifesto of my own inner battle between right and wrong, night and day, good and evil, everything, and nothing at all.

I wandered out after midnight in bare feet, crying, vomiting. Trying to make sense of it all I walked into my uncle's house and woke up my visiting grandmother. The circular spiraling notes—something scribbled about the meaning of life and Ed McMahon. Why was I the only one who understood it? The positive and negative influences everyone has on our general collective state of being? Why was the nature of people to be deceitful, dishonest? I was sick of hearing it, sick of listening to people and their fucking problems and all the petty things they piss and moan about all day long when everything they made they made for themselves. I was tired of lies and ignorance. I was tired of listening to people whine about what they don't have in life when they'd not yet taken time to appreciate what they do have.

How long had I gone on? How long had I been awake? It seemed like forever. My daughter had come and gone. We were supposed to spend her summer vacation together, but she was sent home. I was off the wall. I had visions of ordinary things, and they frightened me. I was seeing the future, and couldn't stop it from coming. I dreamed about things that came to pass, so I began to live in fear of my nightmares. I saw fire in my mother's house, and called to warn her. The fire came within a few weeks. A foster child she was caring for had set fire to his room, my room, the room I grew up in, my inner sanctum.

I started talking in riddles and rhyme. Everything was about hidden meanings, metaphor, codes, visions, predictions. I took things people said in the course of idol chit chat and somehow seemed to know the deeper meaning. People revealed themselves to me on a psychoanalytical level. I learned to keep my observations to myself. People I thought were my "friends" started dropping from my life. No one wanted to hear the truth, and they were all so full of shit, lacking integrity, and blind.

The phone rang. I picked it up, and before even hearing who it was, and I just blurted, "Hey Beth your car broke down didn't it?" I was right. These phenomena occurred with growing frequency. Bits and pieces of intuition, clairvoyance, and premonition snuck into my world.

Beth, my Uncle Don, and my grandmother stood over me as I lay on the couch. I just wanted to rest. I was so tired, had to sleep. I'd been awake for weeks. I wasn't fucking crazy, it was Beth. I tried to tell them that. No one would listen. The look on my grandmother's face was the one thing that brought me back to earth, and I felt myself crawl out from behind Him. Even He knew that there had to be one person to put our faith in when no one could be trusted.

"Will you do this for your old Grandmother?" she pleaded.

Beth and I checked me into Charter Springs Behavioral Health Clinic. The doctor was a quack, and within a day I realized, crazy or not, I had gotten myself into something bad.

Immediately I was given a combination of thyroidazine and tranquilizers. At night I was made to stay in a locked ward, and everything was a mind game. Everything was a play on words and their meanings. The literal breakdown of words unlocked the hidden meaning of their utterances. It was an internal struggle to keep my wits about me. They were determined to steal my soul. It became a vicious game at the point where Dr Bird asked if I felt "stuck" when they drew blood from me that morning. He was implying control over me that he would never have. He had no idea who he was addressing. I realized it was going to be a test of mind games with him. I dug in for battle.

Every patient was given the same regimen. At med pass we all just grabbed a cup-o-pills from the tray—it didn't matter which cup we grabbed, they were all the same. They woke me up in the middle of the night to give me a thick yellow serum that was never identified to me. They kept me locked in a ward with seemingly faceless strangers who were so far out of mind that it was hard to think of them as people, these elderly decaying souls lost to dementia. After the first day I was just staring into space with a big grin on my face. Beth came to see me, and we sat outside in an enclosed area.

"Do you even know where you are?" she asked in tears.

"I'm happy," I replied staring distantly into oblivion. It was all I could do.

A nurse rushed us saying that I was forbidden to be outside. Why?

An old woman slumped in a Gerri-Chair mindlessly staring at the floor grabbed my arm as I passed her, and she sat up suddenly, looked right at me. Her eyes brighten, and for a moment she seemed coherent, full of light.

"You are a good man," She rasps. "Good," she says loudly, and touched my arm with her bony leather fingers. Her eyes clouded over, her body drooled back into a lifeless slump.

My second night there I went into my room at bed time, and everything was moved opposite of how it had been the night before. There was a grizzled, fetid old man lying in my bed. I brought it to the attention of the nurses, and they laughed and said it was my roommate and to go back to my room. The other bed in the room stank. I stripped the sheets and lay on the bare mattress.

They told Beth I was a compulsive liar, and that she had a problem with co-dependence. At that point she knew they were full of shit because my integrity was the characteristic that drew her to me. They were telling me that she didn't want me bothering her with phone calls and telling her I was happy there and didn't need her in my life. They tried to invoke the Baker Act on me, but I was too strong. It was three days of head games and tip-toeing around the doctor's transparent inferior mentality. He was trying to keep me there for the purpose of exploiting my Medicare benefits. I was sure of it. I suspected Beth of being part of the plot. They were working us against each other, but we were too strong. They stopped putting her calls through to me. Who did they think they were fucking with? No, we were not the mindless minions of complacent society content to be manipulated, content to believe someone's words just because they're a doctor. We knew better than that.

"I'm looking for a mathematician." "I need a mathematician." I wandered the halls telling everyone. I saw myself in places unfamiliar but frighteningly real: whitewashed classroom, a studio with wrap around windows. I envisioned Beth and I kept apart by a force beyond our control—fate, destiny. I saw classrooms; I interpreted them to be government reeducation camps. I saw it all as things I was being forced into. The force was nature. There was no way to fight it. My unlived life unraveled, flickering through my head—snap shots from the album, I lost my mind, unadulterated fear—body-snatchers.

Two guys who appeared to be patients started asking questions about whom I knew and where I go around Lake Weir. They had names, places. Narcotics officers were doggin' me? Too creepy. They knew where I lived and who I knew in the neighborhood. They were digging for something, looking for me to say something particular, but it never got that far. They found me alone in a room and we started talking.

"You mean you really were in an accident?" They were astonished, like I hadn't been through the story several times before.

Then it hit me . . . The bastards. The people they thought I was associated with, the people they wanted to know about—cocaine. It explained why they had Beth include a baggie of laundry soap with my personal items. They assumed I was another common cocaine case, and were waiting to see if I would snort the detergent. They had no idea what they were doing.

I stood at a pay phone, doped up, trying to remember my phone number, but couldn't get it to come. Time after time I tried, growing more frustrated and desperate with every failed attempt. Sometimes I made it five numbers through sometimes only two. Finally after being reduced to tears He took over and pushed the seven numbers.

Beth and I were able to compare notes on what was being said and what I was going through inside. She was conflicted about what to do: listen to the doctor, or listen to the crazy boyfriend. Despite the fact that I needed help we agreed on one thing. I had to get out of there before they pushed me to the "other side" (as the doctor called it). In our circle talk I took to mean a straight jacket and more drugs than I would be able to recover from, though I wasn't going to let that happen without hurting someone in the process. He was immune to tranquilizers.

It was frightening to be a wounded animal as I was. The only means of survival I possessed was to go for the throat. He was aware of that and I knew He knew I knew it. We were both okay with it because if ever He had the need to kill or be killed, I would be out of the equation all together, and I would want Him there to do what had to be done.

I was told by the Quack I was not allowed to leave. I was being kept against my will. I started auditing the place like I was on the front line working in the healthcare industry again. I pointed out violations of safety codes and policies. I pointed out practices that were illegal—fire code violations, foodservice violations. I reduced a nurse to tears by preying on her moral conscious.

"Are you proud of what it is you do here? How can you live with yourself knowing what goes on in this place? You're sicker than I am."

Others were taunting, sarcastic.

"No there's no earthquakes yet," they laughed.

Still, they acknowledged I was able to generate a following. When we lined up to move as a group I walked back from arts and crafts with a demented elderly holding my arm. Everyone else, young and old alike, followed behind. No matter how slowly I went, no one walked ahead. It was the full blown Jesus complex.

"They really do follow him though," I heard a nurse exclaim. I looked back and everyone was following, like a procession. It was an omnipotent occurrence.

I only made it out of there alive because Beth was on the outside raising hell and ready with the police if they would not let me leave. I was a voluntary patient and could walk out the door at any time. They had no legal ground to hold me, but I knew fighting would only give them the grounds. Inside, I sat in a chair under a poster of the patient's bill of rights and locked my feet around its legs.

"I know how to read and I know exactly what this all means," I told the staff. I was leaving that day whether they liked it or not.

Immediately prior to being discharged I sat in the office with Dr. Bird as he pushed buttons, trying to get me to swing, trying to provoke violence. I talked circles around his simple head, signed the papers, and I left. He was hardly a worthy adversary. There was one last test, to retrieve my bags. They were in a closet set off in a kitchenette, and the door had a bolt so that it could be locked from the outside. I knew what it was for. On my first day in the place one of the two guys who I suspected to be narcs bolted his friend in the kitchenette and he dramatically panicked banging on the glass screaming "Let me out, Let me out." After a minute they laughed, but I took it as a warning. A nurse accompanied me and I hesitated before entering. I was hesitant about going through the door—scared shitless actually. She reassured me that it was OK, but I was leery just the same. I didn't trust anyone. I was ready for a fight. If she made one step back toward the door I was going to plow through her like a Mack Truck. Inside the kitchenette the nurse unlocked a closet. Bags and suitcases were piled in on top of each other, like no one was ever intended to leave. Whose bags were at the bottom? I found mine on top of the heap, grabbed them, and made haste about getting out of there.

I got home to find all the windows covered with blankets, the sunlight barely seeping in around the edges. My house was a dark and surreal place, like someplace in a dream. The first thing I did was call James, my surrogate sense of security. He told me about someone he knew who also sought help from Charter in North Carolina. The day he finally fought free of their prison he went home, got his truck, and drove it right through the front door. He too had mentioned a thick nasty yellow serum that kept him in a drooling daze; the tranquilizer they give you in your sleep.

Charter Springs had the reputation for tactics in trapping innocent people and drugging them into displaying mental conditions they didn't have. They turned people into zombies and, my hunch was right, to exploit them for Medicare/Medicaid payments. Everything I saw inside supported this, and it sent me into a spiral of paranoia.

I booby trapped my garage with trip wires and obstacles. Anyone evacuating the attic would have to run straight through it, and I would be there to watch them fall. They were up there listening to me, watching, tapping my phone. I pulled the pin and threw a grenade through the opening in the ceiling. They came pouring out. I was in full-blown war mode. Survival of the fittest, kill or be killed. The bug fogger filled the attic with droplets of chemical death, but no one emerged from the attic.

I watched my boat-house through the window. There was a door cut into the earth below it. The Ocala National Forrest was on fire, and I knew why it was burning—insurgents. The government was burning out the pockets of foreign nationals that had taken up residence and were planning to make the forest a base of operations for the invasion. They all wore black fatigues and ninja masks as they emerged from the boat house crouched in single file. They carried automatic weapons.

Late at night I conducted fire-drills. I had hoses run throughout the yard in case the flames came near. I soaked the roof at night so when the time came I would be ready. I wasn't sleeping, but on constant vigilant readiness. I separated my world into two categories—them and us. I was determined to sort them for myself.

I hadn't slept in more than a week. I was on a mission with no objective. I was at war and everything became war. The earth was blanketed in a murky purple haze, like some kind of chemical death. I suddenly knew what Hendrix was singing about. I had visions about ranks of soldiers marching. I began calling everyone from my past; those who had wronged me or wronged others. I preached to them about the error of their ways. I began calling people out on their lies, I could see through everything. I had a built in bullshit detector and I wasn't afraid to use it. I was adamant about honesty in myself and in others, and I refused to associate myself with anyone or anything that didn't carry with it a positive aura. A sniper watches me from the roof of the house next door.

I came to believe that my accident wasn't an accident at all. I saw an eighteen-wheeler in front of me and the back door flew open. A ramp came down and it slammed on the brakes. My bike sped up the ramp and

I was locked in the back of the truck while two guys beat me with iron pipes. The horror of it hit me as real as anything I had been through. Fighter planes corkscrewed in the clouds over head—the only way I could explain the vortex, like an inverted tornado in the sky.

Beth paid Chaz from the music store to stay with me, to make sure I didn't go off on anything too crazy while she was at school. She blamed the Amway tapes that my uncle peddled—subliminal self-help propaganda. I had no need of their advice. It was too late, I was over the edge. I became completely engrossed in the fantasy of it. Chaz, who was supposed to be looking out for me, became engrossed in my "missions." I escorted him around the greater Ocala area taking care of business that didn't exist and doing things that never got done.

My leg infected and I sought care at a local orthopedic clinic where the first thing I was told after getting an X-ray was the leg had to be amputated. The small clinics in Florida were frightening like that, and I used to joke as we drove past them, tucked into sprawling communities of mauve, stucco, and Spanish tile. "That looks like one of those places where you go in for an appendectomy and they sell your kidney." I wasn't going to accept their assessment of my leg.

I immediately got on the phone with Dr. Acker, and he agreed that it would have been a tragedy if I agreed with their assessment of the situation. He told me of a similar instance with doctors in the same area known as "The Villages." They were going to put a woman under the knife to remove something that had been misread in an X-ray. Luckily, he had his own associates give a second opinion. It seemed like playing with one's own life to blindly seek medical attention in my neck of the woods. Incompetence was all around me—maddening, sad.

I went back to Halifax Medical in Daytona for another operation, and they immediately admitted me. A baseball-sized lump of abscess had grown under the scar on my hip. My body rejected the rod that was embedded in the femur, and it had to be removed.

My hair was long, ratty, and starting to dread. While in the hospital Beth shaved my head using an entire bag of disposable Bic razors. It was a maddening loss of identity—I barely had one in the first place—to suddenly have no hair. The lingering warning from Dr. Acker haunted me. The infection could return at any time. Losing the leg was always possible.

I spent the next year living with a Hickman catheter embedded in my subclavian vein—a white coil of surgical tubing pinned to my chest. Every day I went to an infectious disease clinic. Vancomyacin and Rocephin dripped into my body, and the catheter was flushed with Heparin, thinning my blood to water so that even trace amounts of things like household cleaners felt like poison inside me. I could taste them in my blood, on my tongue. I sprayed some W-D 40 in the garage one afternoon and I thought I was going to die. I was growing weaker each day. I was slowly being put to death and couldn't take it any more. I had to get that thing out of me. I thought it was part of a grand eradication plot against me.

Beth and I were driving home from shopping as the sun was setting. Tears streaming down my face, I pulled on the catheter trying to rip it from my vein, pulling on the hose, screaming, "Just you and me to the end baby,"

Nothing. No blood, no pain. No sweet kiss of death. It just stretched to my knees and snapped back.

We'd been to see several psychiatrists in search of help, but none of them told me what I wanted to hear. After Charter I was deathly afraid of medication and had no trust of doctors. I tried Depakote, but it only made me sick and gave me a rash. It was the last thing I was willing to try. They all wanted me to have their own brand of "counseling." When I asked, "Why do I need counseling?" I was told, so I could have some direction in my life. Despite the manic breakdown, I was more directed with regard to my own future than anyone I'd ever known. I'd seen it in a nut-shell.

I had a scar on my forehead I called the mark of Cain. It started just above the eyebrow and disappeared beneath my hairline. I was looking at a possible diagnosis of Bi-polar disorder, but no one was ruling out the crack to the head as being the culprit. In fact, before leaving Halifax hospital after the accident, Dr Acker warned me about the possibility of a PTSD breakdown.

I was euphoric and high on life, love, and liberty one moment, wrought with despair, depression, agony the next. The word bipolar—it's one thing to say it, but still another to live through it. It's horror at its worst, and sadness like you'll never know. When it comes to a manic episode, just because the sky isn't really falling doesn't necessarily mean that pieces of it won't hurt when they land on your head. All things I experienced were driven by real time emotion, action, and reaction. It wasn't all psychotic delirium; there were truths revealed that only a mad person can know. My mind and soul existed inside me as matter is to antimatter. They could not exist on the same plane together. My mind exploded.

I decided to take a trip north again. With Dakota and all my Amway shit in the back of my pick-up, I left in February. I stopped in South Carolina to visit Kirk, but he wasn't there when I arrived. I found him at work the next morning, said a quick hello, then headed to North Carolina to see James. I spent the night with him and Dianne and continued the next morning.

By the time I got to my mother's house in Mass I'd lost a day. It might have been in Hartford where I had a dim memory of being confused about which way to go. I might have spent an entire day driving in a circle not realizing what I had done. I couldn't be sure.

I was shooting hoops with the foster child my mother was caring for, and she watched from the picture window with her tenant/boyfriend, Bill. He latched onto her the day my father left. The two of them were using the foster kid to create the illusion of a happy family, and the dumb smiles on their two faces in the window that day prompted that disastrous collision of mind and soul.

I spiraled. Neither my mother nor Bill had the facets to be raising a troubled adolescent. He was a paycheck to them, and that was the only way I could see it. Bill was a manipulative passive aggressive who used a heart condition as an excuse for everything. Ma was still reeling from the trauma my father had dumped on her life, and Bill was skillfully using that to his advantage. Someone had to see it for her.

I purchased a brand new vehicle for my mother to help her get back on her feet when my father left her with nothing, and it had come to the point where she was checking with Bill to see if she could use it. I was furious. His motives and intentions were transparent. He was a leech, a grubby little parasite, but nothing I could do or say would remedy the problem. She was blind.

That night I kicked in the door to his apartment, the apartment where my grandmother used to live. My mother was so proud of Bill because he was going to go to clown college. Was this for real? With fire in my eyes and hell in my voice I told him I had a bullet with his name on it. I watched the fear on his face and thought if I glared just a little bit harder, and if his face got just a little bit whiter, I could push his heart into arrest. I left the house before the police arrived. I had been awake for days.

I stayed with my cousin Dave and his family that night. The next morning, after maybe an hour of sleep, I told them I was going to work. I decided to drop in on someone I knew from high school who lived in the area. No one was home. I then proceeded on a mission that found me breaking into someone's house looking for secret documents. All I found was an NRA ball cap. It looked official, so I put it on.

I took a briefcase I found in a car at yet another house, and there was a list of names inside—another pyramid.

I knocked on the door of a state trooper who wasn't home and, playing the part of an inquisitive detective, asked the woman who answered the door about people and things. I told her to let her husband know that big brother was watching him. I had no fear of big brother, because I *was* big brother.

I spent the rest of the day driving around dropping in on people I remembered from my past. Some were glad to see me, and some were scared as hell. I euphorically spun donuts in the street for what could have been a minute, or five. I was seeking terminal velocity. I ran around in my truck all day chasing distant garble on my CB radio calling, may-day, may-day.

I looked for pockets of survivors. I kept keying in (SOS) to reach anyone out there, anyone at all. I tried to speak out from behind the madman, but He pushed me back inside.

I went looking for the K-9 college, the kennel where I got Dakota, but forgot where it was, and along the way I saw a ninja standing on the sidewalk. That was my sign. I was back in the war, so I stopped into a bank. Something I saw triggered the knowledge that it was the bank I had to go into. I spoke to a woman at a desk. I was looking for something in accordance with the LMSHA (Lost Morals Sheep Herders Association), which was something I was let in on earlier that day by Doc, an old friend I'd visited. She looked at me like I was crazy, so I just thanked her for her time and walked out.

Every time I looked up in the rear view mirror I saw someone I knew in the car behind me. My back-up—faces from the past. I found my way back to my mother's house. Beth was on her way from Florida. She was the only person who could bring me back, the only person I trusted, but it was too late. I kept thinking I heard the car pull into the driveway, but every time I got up to see—nothing. Over and over I heard the tires crunch on the pebbled driveway and the car door open and close, but then nothing. I couldn't hold on any longer. I wanted so much to feel the acceleration, the warp, the velocity of moving through the light.

I want to go back there, calm in the silence of my own pure energy, but I am dead, trapped on earth in an afterlife where I do not belong. My mind fights to break through the confusion, and now inside these walls, these cold, pale, yellow tile walls, my only hope is Him. He is my last chance for salvation.